# Gloucestershire
# Walks with Children

## Juliet Greenwood

SIGMA
Leisure

**Copyright** © Juliet Greenwood, 1997

**Published by** Sigma Leisure – an imprint of
Sigma Press, 1 South Oak Lane, Wilmslow, Cheshire SK9 6AR, England.

**British Library Cataloguing in Publication Data**
A CIP record for this book is available from the British Library.

**ISBN:** 1-85058-587-3

**Typesetting and Design by:** Sigma Press, Wilmslow, Cheshire.

**Cover photograph:** Maisie and Meredith climbing to the Devil's Chimney, Leckhampton Hill, Gloucestershire (Gwyn Richards)

**Maps and illustrations:** William Greenwood

**Printed by:** MFP Design & Print

**Disclaimer:** the information in this book is given in good faith and is believed to be correct at the time of publication. No responsibility is accepted by either the author or publisher for errors or omissions, or for any loss or injury howsoever caused. Only you can judge your own fitness, competence and experience.

# Preface

As a newcomer to the county of Gloucestershire, I cannot claim to be an expert on its history and wildlife. But what a way to discover it! And discovery is the essence of this book.

Gloucestershire's terrain and habitats and its long history make it a great county to explore with children. Together we discovered woods and meadows, river banks and canal sides. Each walk has something of interest to distinguish it, whether it be a man-made construction or nature's own beauty in a pond or a wood.

The detailed directions will, hopefully, help children to keep going because there will always be something to look for up ahead. They can stretch their minds as well as their legs by identifying flowers, trees, butterflies and birds, and answering the questions. Where applicable the season has been noted so that you'll know what to see and when to see it.

I hope you will also discover that your children are capable of walking much further than you might have thought. This book should help parents help their children to find out that walking can be fun and encourage them to get out there into the wide open spaces and discover the environment. It's also a much cheaper leisure activity than most on offer.

Some of the walks may have elements that you do not consider to be so child-friendly, like a narrow bridge or a steep flight of rough-hewn steps but remember, to your children the only limit is their imagination and if those vines look like jungle creepers, then you had better watch out for tigers! Children enjoy a challenge and I know my own will walk a mile for a stile to climb.

I hope you will revive the lost art of walking in the next generation and through your explorations now, instil an interest in, and love for the countryside that will last them a lifetime.

# Acknowledgements

To my Gran, who walked with me.

I owe a big debt of thanks to my husband William and children Maisie and Meredith, without whom it would have been impossible to do this book; to my parents-in-law, Sue and David, who were, quite simply, brilliant and came through with valuable help on many occasions; and to my own parents, Mum for her computing skills, support and advice, and Dad for his legal eye and enthusiasm. Thanks also to Gwyn for the cover photo and being a constant source of information, and to the various friends who accompanied us on walks. Your support was much appreciated.

*Juliet Greenwood*

# *Contents*

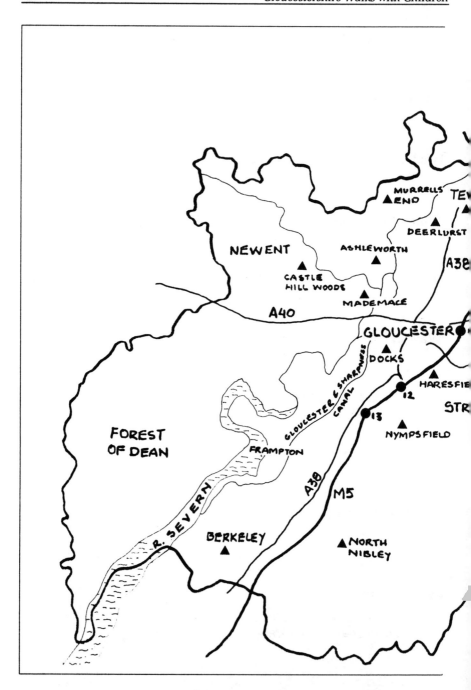

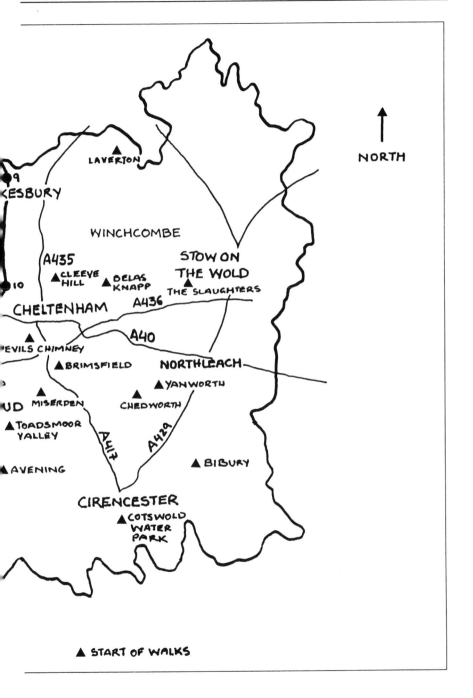

NORTH

LAVERTON

▲9
KESBURY

WINCHCOMBE

A435

STOW ON
THE WOLD

▲CLEEVE
HILL
▲DELAS
KNAPP
▲
THE SLAUGHTERS

▲10

CHELTENHAM  A436

A40

EVILS CHIMNEY

▲BRIMSFIELD

NORTHLEACH

▲YANWORTH

UD  ▲MISERDEN

▲
CHEDWORTH

▲TOADSMOOR
YALLEY

A417

A429

▲AVENING

▲BIBURY

CIRENCESTER

▲COTSWOLD
WATER
PARK

▲ START OF WALKS

# Introduction

There are twenty-five walks in this book, none of them more than four miles long, the majority just two or three. As a guideline to how far your child might walk, it may be helpful to know that we did the walks with a two and a half year old, who needed the occasional shoulder ride, and a six year old who must have walked 99% of the distance each time. Short and sweet is really the key to a successful walk with children.

The walks cover all sorts of surfaces and some have some quite steep climbs on them, but nothing that ours could not cope with. Unfortunately, few of the routes are suitable for pushchairs. If they were, they probably wouldn't be so much fun, as children enjoy narrow paths, stiles, bridges and steps. Where a short section along a lane is mentioned, be assured that it is a very quiet country lane or has adequate verges.

What you see with regards to animal and plant life depends on you but hopefully our hints tell you where to look and when. The black and white illustrations throughout the book are to aid with identification of certain species.

Finally, I apologise to any family without a car as I have assumed that everyone will reach the starting point for each walk by that particular mode of transport.

### Typestyle Conventions

To make this book easy to use by both parents and children, we have chosen three different type-styles:

**"Bold" text, just like this,** to give directions for the adults.

☺ Plain text with a smiley face to pick out interesting features of the walk for children (& grown ups too!) We use the same style for quiz questions.

Smaller, script-style, text like this for background information.

Now for the walks!

# The Devil's Chimney – Leckhampton Hill

A steep hill climb up to far-reaching views. Take a pair of binoculars and see what you can see. Over the brow and jutting out from the edge is the Devil's Chimney. "Not much of a chimney," said Maisie, "there's no hole for the smoke to come out of." A good point, but it is an interesting rock formation with a very romantic name. Decide for yourself what it could be and what it should be called. Small children may find the steep paths difficult.

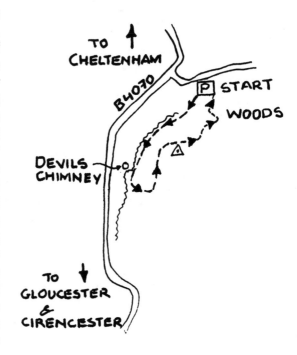

---

**Starting point:**  Leckhampton Hill. There is a car park for the hill off Daisybank Road, which is off the B4070 out of Cheltenham, towards Cirencester.

**Distance:**  2 miles

**Terrain:**  Very steep hills, woodland paths and open grasslands.

**Map:**  O.S. Landranger 163

No public toilets, no refreshments and not suitable for pushchairs.

---

1. **Look for the stone opposite the entrance of the car park which says Leckhampton Hill Walk. Follow this path.**

☺ Look out for adders! The adder is Britain's only venomous snake. The male is pale grey with dark zigzag stripes. Females are duller but larger.

**Common Adder**

2. **The path climbs up the hill, getting quite steep. Take care.**

☺ Look out for the numbered stone markers. Number 2 should be coming up.

3. **The path emerges into a clearing with the ruins of a stone hut. Follow the arrow on marker Number 3.**

4. **The path forks ahead. Go right.**

☺ It is very steep and slippery so be careful as you climb or you may slide all the way back down to the bottom.

5.  **At the top of this climb is a small plateau with fantastic views across the trees. Take a breather and have a look around.**

6.  **Onward and upward, straight through the trees and out on to a rocky clearing and along the outer path to a bench. Sit and admire the view.**

Q: How many church spires can you count?

7.  **Continue along the edge. Just over the brow is the Devil's Chimney.**

☺ The 'chimney' was created by the cutting of a tramway down the hillside for quarrying purposes.

8.  **Follow the main path away from the edge. At the top turn left at the arrowed post. At the fork go right across the grass.**

**The Devil's Chimney**

☺ Across the grass, to the left, is a stone mound with a topograph on it. This tells you the direction of the things you can see across the valley.

9. **Walk away from the topograph across to another man-made structure.**

☺ As you pass a bench on the left, look at the plaque next to it.

Q: Who is being welcomed to the world?

The other structure is called a triangulation point and is used for making maps.

10. **Follow the narrow path down from the triangulation point towards a gate or go back to the main path and pass stone marker Number 5.**

☺ What happened to stone marker Number 4?!

11. **This bit is tricky as there are many paths criss-crossing about. Go straight on past the gate then turn left down one of the paths so that you are heading out towards the edge and a bench. Turn right down a narrow path that goes into the trees. Fork right.**

☺ You should pass stone marker Number 6. Look out for butterflies in the summer.

12. **Go straight ahead and pass a post with an arrow on it on your left. Pass a gate and a bridle path on the right. Continue straight on the main path. Pass an uprooted footpath sign and follow its arrow to the left.**

13. **The path dips down into the trees. Keep on the lower path.**

☺ Scout ahead for the marker at the bottom, Number 7.

14. **Turn right at the bottom. Pass a wall with a steep drop on the other side. Continue straight ahead.**

**15. At the path crossroads go left, then fork right back to the car park.**

☺ Did you see any adders? They hibernate in winter. They have large fangs and are slow-moving but will put in a fast disappearing act if you should approach, probably long before you even see them.

# 𝒯he 𝒮ecret 𝒫ond – 𝒞astle 𝒽ill 𝒲oods

This is a walk of narrow, winding woodland paths leading you through dark trees and then out into the light, to a secret pond. At the time of year we did the walk, early June, every green stem was occupied by a damsel fly. These are similar to dragonflies, only smaller and electric blue in colour. It was the mating season. There were so many of them that it was easy to get close to several at a time, they may even land briefly upon you. Look also for dragonflies and other pond wildlife. You may find orchids growing on the far bank. Here is nature in all its glory, a truly magical walk. Wellies are recommended for all.

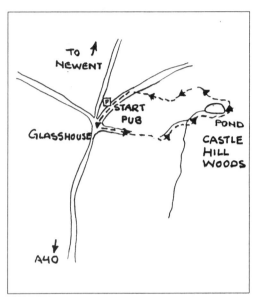

**Starting point:** Glasshouse. This is a tiny hamlet near Newent Woods. Take the A40 to Ross on Wye out of Gloucester and take the right turn to Glasshouse off it. Parking is available off the road opposite the pub, The Glasshouse.

**Distance:** 1½ miles

**Terrain:** Woodland paths, could be muddy and overgrown after rain.

**Map:** Landranger 162

**Public Toilets:** No

**Refreshments:** Pub at the starting point, with garden

1. **Walk past the pub and take the footpath on the left.**

☺ Notice the hedge shaped like a house opposite the pub.

Q: What are the men on the pub sign doing? The clue is in the name.

2. **Walk down the track, pass a house on the left and enter the woods. At the fork, go left.**

☺ Can you hear sounds of water?

3. **Go under a post which is intended to stop horses using the path, and at the arrows take the left path down.**

☺ Listen to the sounds of the wood.

4. **Follow the path and at a fork go left. The narrow path then joins a wider one. Turn left along it.**

5. **The path then dips down next to a stream which forks in two different directions. Follow the path to the stream fork and cross the right-hand stream. It is narrower here.**

☺ There is no bridge so how will you get across? Can you jump it? Are there stepping stones? Can you wade in your wellies? Or will a grown-up lift you over?

6. **Once safely across, follow the path to a T-junction. Turn left. Up ahead the tiny stream has become a large pond. Follow the path out into the open and see what you can see.**

☺ Look for bulrushes, dragonflies, damselflies, fish, orchids, pond skaters, frogs. Anything else? A very rickety bridge leads to a tiny island — for very intrepid explorers only!

Ponds are ideal habitats for studying food chains. Water plants feed the herbivores, e.g. water snails, and then the carnivores, e.g. newts and sticklebacks, snap up the herbivores! Pond skaters hunt on the surface for any insects that become trapped in the surface film. The skaters rely on surface tension to 'walk on water'. They have to be careful of a hungry fish down below though. The Common Blue Damselfly is found in the vegetation around ponds and is most active between May and September. The male is blue and the female is green. They are smaller and daintier than dragonflies and slower flyers.

**Damselfly**

Dragonflies are fierce hunters. True dragonflies are divided into two groups, hawkers and darters. Hawkers spend most of their time in the air searching for prey. Darters rest and pounce. Dragonflies and their larvae are a popular food in the Far East. Yuck!!

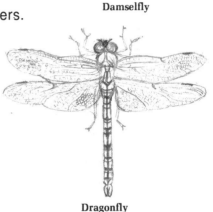

**Dragonfly**

Orchids are one of the largest plant families with over 17 000 species. Many are noted for their exotic flowers.

7. Follow the path around the pond to the edge of an open field. Follow the path out into the field but then turn immediately left to re-enter woods. Take the path on the right, which climbs steadily up the hill.

8. Turn left at the path crossroads. The path climbs steadily.

☺ Look down on beautiful trees below. It is a mixed deciduous wood so there are many different types of trees.

9. At the end of the path is a yellow footpath arrow pointing straight out into an open field. The path is marked on the map as going straight across this field, but if the grass is too long

then it is hard to follow. Alternatively, turn right and walk along the top edge of the field, following the line of the hedge. Go down the far side and turn right approximately three quarters of the way along.

10. The track leads out on to a lane. Turn left, and round the bend should be the car.

### Other Attractions

Nearby in Newent is the National Birds of Prey Centre which is a brilliant day out for all the family. There is a collection of birds of prey and regular flying demonstrations. Open February to November. Admission charge.

# A Pleasant Walk through a Pheasant Wood – Miserden

Firstly, you will walk through the pretty village of Miserden, with its many old houses and features. Miserden is a 'proper' village, with a pub, post office/shop, school and church. Look for names and dates on the houses. Once through the village, you enter Miserden park with some superb forest views and then go into the woods themselves. This is where you are likely to see pheasants. Make this an autumn walk and there

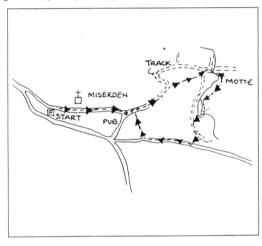

should be plenty to see. Look out for brooks and bridges, winding paths and forest tracks, pheasants and feeders. There is also a large pond so you may see swans and ducks as well.

---

**Starting point:**   Miserden village. Miserden is between Birdlip and Bisley. If you take the B4070 out of Birdlip and then turn left towards Whiteway, Miserden is only a little further. If you approach from this direction you will find a public car park on the right immediately as you enter the village, just before the village school.

**Distance:**   2 miles

**Map:**   O.S.Landranger 163

**Terrain:**   Narrow woodland paths, short sections on quiet lanes, some hills.

**Refreshments:**   Shop and pub in village.

---

1. **Turn right out of the car park and walk through the village.**

☺ Look for the interesting design on the school gate. Outside the village shop is a strange black object. Do you know what it was? Look out for the war memorial.

2. **Go past the war memorial and the entrance to the church.**

☺ The church dates back to Saxon times so it is approximately 900 years old. It is very beautiful inside, with cool stone walls and warm wooden pews. The stained glass windows are not very big but very bright. Look up at the barn-like roof.

3. **Turn left at the tree with the sheltered bench built around it, in the centre of the village (to the right is the pub). Follow a sign to the nursery.**

Q: Do you think the tree grew out of the roof of the bench shelter?

4. **Continue straight ahead.**

☺ Look carefully at the houses in the village. Many of them have dates on them.

You should pass another strange black object. Do you know what it is yet?

5. **At the gate marked 'Private', go through the small gate to the left of it. There is a footpath sign just before it. Follow the "road".**

☺ Scout ahead and look out for a large tree on the right of the path with a green arrow and a picture of the tree from the village on it.

6. **Turn right across the grass at the tree, just before the 'road' starts to bend to the left. Head towards the drystone wall. About**

**halfway along is a yellow arrow by a stone stile. Go over the
stile and into the wood.**

☺ You are now in the Pheasant Wood. How many pheasants
will you see?

Pheasant

Pheasants were introduced from Asia in ancient times. They are
semi-domesticated as they are usually under the protection of a
gamekeeper during the breeding season, for hunting later in the
year. They nest on the ground and are reluctant to fly, but will do
so if disturbed.

7.  **Follow the path through the woods and down to the 'road'.**

☺ Look out for green arrows on trees.

8.  **Go straight over the 'road', down another 'road' and over a
    bridge. Follow the green arrow to the right, past a "No Horses"
    sign and into the wood.**

☺ Keep looking for pheasants.

Also, run ahead to find a tiny bridge.

9.  **Cross the bridge and follow the narrow, rooty path. When the narrow path reaches a wider one, turn right.**

☺ Look out for the next green arrow. It's around the corner of the wide path.

10. **Follow the arrow round to the left and out into a clearing. Continue straight ahead.**

☺ Just up ahead is a large pond so look out for ducks and maybe even swans, or, if you are very lucky, herons.

11. **Follow the path through the trees, alongside the pond. It is a narrow path, up and down over roots, so take care.**

12. **The path opens out at the edge of the pond, next to a bench. Continue straight, over a floodgate.**

Q:  Can you hear sounds of rushing water?

13. **Opposite is a tree with an arrow on it. Follow it to the left. (Ignore the green arrow pointing right.)**

☺ Pass a pheasant feeder on the left.

Q:  What do pheasants eat?

14. **The path climbs up. Turn right at the top, across open grass, and then go up a track to a gate.**

☺ There is another pheasant feeder on the left before the gate.

15. **Go through the gate and straight across the field to another.**

☺ Your Mum and Dad might like to look at the beautiful big house over to the right!

16. Go through the gate and right, out on to the lane. Walk down the lane to a footpath which is on the right just before the telephone wires post. Go over a stone stile and walk alongside the wall.

☺ In autumn look for conkers.

Horse chestnut trees have leaves that look like hands. The 'horse' part of the name comes from the Turks who used the tree as medicine for horses. The tree was introduced in the 16th century so conker collecting has only been possible here for the last 400 years!

17. Go over another stone stile and past some houses and back into the village. Turn left, then right at the tree and retrace steps 2 and 1 back to the car park.

# Light The Way – Haresfield Beacon

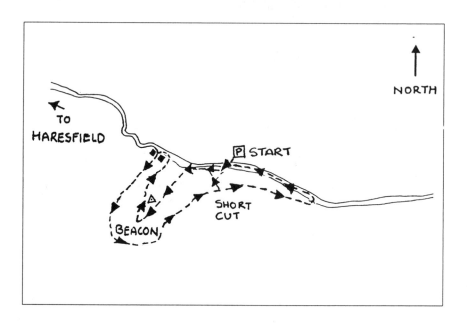

This is another popular spot so you are likely to meet other walkers and dogs up here. But there is enough view for everyone. There is no actual evidence of the beacon itself, but it is easy to imagine where it would have been. Beacons were lit to warn of enemy invasion and here is the perfect vantage point. The River Severn shimmers in the distance and all the world seems to lie before it. On a clear day you can see for 75 miles.

**Starting point:**   Haresfield is between Hardwicke and Stonehouse. At the top of Ring Hill, out of Haresfield, there is a parking area.

**Distance:**   3 miles

**Map:**   O.S. Landranger 162

**Terrain:**   Grassy tracks, short section on quiet lane.

1. **Follow the Cotswold Way sign to the right so that you initially walk parallel to the road.**

☺ Almost immediately the views open up to the left. Can you see the River Severn?

2. **Go through a gate or the gap in the wall next to it, and follow the path through the trees and then alongside a field to a stile. Keep straight ahead.**

☺ Over the stile is the site of an ancient fort. It is just lumps and bumps now. Imagine your invaders coming across the valley and having to climb that hill to attack.

The Celts fortified hill tops with ditches and ramparts. They were places of refuge in war time, but also in general use for administration centres and livestock enclosures. A 3rd century Roman camp occupied the extreme point. An early British camp was above it.

3. **Go carefully down a small slope. On the right is a triangulation point.**

☺ Triangulation points are used by map-makers to help make maps accurate.

Can you see the Tyndale Monument over on the far hill? Can you see the motorway? And the railway line?

4. **Walk out to the edge and look out on the Vale of Gloucester.**

☺ This is probably where the beacon would have been lit. During the 15th century a chain of hilltop fires were lit as signals to the British of the Spanish invasion. The beacon signal could spread the news quicker than a messenger on horseback.

5. **From the trig' point, go right and walk round the of the fort. Continue so that you are walking away from the edge towards a stile.**

☺ Look for rabbits.

It was the Normans who introduced the rabbit to Britain. Rabbits are well known for their ability to reproduce. One doe can produce thirty young in eight months. Their young are born underground, blind and naked. This is very different to hares, a close relative. Their young are born above ground and have fur and can see. Rabbits are widespread in grassland and live in groups. Listen for their warning thumps and look for the white flash of their tails as they see you approaching.

Q: Can you name two enemies of the rabbit?

A: Foxes, stoats, birds of prey, humans.

6. **The path continues alongside a fence, with woods to the left. Continue along the track.**

☺ Look for the yellow arrow on the marker stone and a footpath sign on the tree.

7. **Follow the track down the hill and over a stile by a gate. Then pass through the gap by the second gate. Take care as this emerges on to the lane.**

8. **Turn left and then left again into the farmyard.**

☺ Look for cows in the barn on the right. But do not go in.

9. **Walk straight through the yard, through the gate and past the barn next to the house, going into the field. Then go through the gate on the right. It is marked by footpath signs.**

10. **Walk diagonally across the field to the bottom corner and over a stile. Turn left and follow the track. Go through a gateway marked by a blue post and on alongside a fence to another gateway. Turn left.**

11. **Walk across the field, passing a metal manger.**

Q: What do you think the round metal structure in the middle of the field is for?

12. Go through a wooden gate and straight on past another manger. A narrow path becomes apparent which gets wider through the trees. Continue straight across the field.

13. Go straight past a stile on the right and continue straight ahead.

☺ The path is now skirting around the bottom of the hill, at the top of which is the fort where you were just standing. So now you are in the position of the enemy. Would you like to have to climb that hill and have to fight at the top?

14. The path runs alongside a drystone wall and starts to climb. It then runs down to a stile. Continue straight.

☺ On the left along here is a *short cut*. Follow this path up to some steep steps which emerge at the car parking area.

15. Climb over another stile by a gate.

☺ On the left is a stone bench.

16. Continue past two huge beech trees then the top comes into view. Turn left at the arrowed post at the top and go through the gap in the wall out on to the lane. Turn left and walk down the quiet lane to the parking area.

**Beech Leaf**

# *Exploration Brimpsfield!*

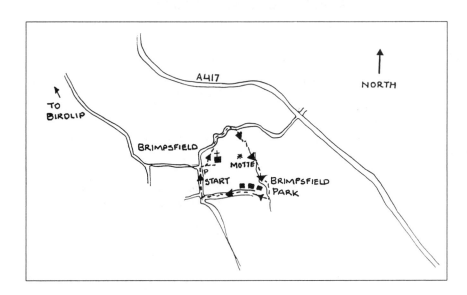

Although without a main focus, this is an interesting walk. It covers varying terrain and paths have to be found and followed through many twists and dips. There are gates, stiles, stepping stones and bridges to conquer. Up and down, over and under.

---

**Starting point:**  Brimpsfield village. The village is one and a quarter miles on from Birdlip, which can be found off the A417 to Cirencester. Take the B4070 after the Air Balloon roundabout and follow signs to Birdlip and Brimpsfield. Park in the village, where the road widens opposite the war memorial.

**Distance:**  2 miles

**Terrain:**  Fields, woods and tracks. Short section on a quiet lane.

**Map:**  O.S. Landranger 163

**Refreshments:**  Pub and shop in nearby Birdlip.

---

1.  The path is across the road from the war memorial, in the corner. Follow signs to the church. Go through the gate with 'To The Church' written on it and follow the concrete path.

2.  As you round the corner and the church comes into sight, there is a visible beaten path through the grass, on the left, to a stile in a drystone wall. This is the way to go but have a look at the church first.

☺ Go into the churchyard and through the yew archways. It is a simple Norman church, which makes it about 800 years old. Look at the simplicity of the stonework next to the bright colours of the windows.

In the churchyard, look at the yew trees. The leaves and seeds of the yew are poisonous to humans and animals. The oldest living trees in Britain are probably yews, some may be 1500 years old. You cannot count the rings on a felled tree though because yew trees become hollow with age. Yew wood was traditionally used for archers' longbows as it bends without splitting. Look for lichen on the headstones. It will only grow in churchyards with clean air as lichen is very sensitive to pollution.

3.  Climb over the stile and follow the path straight across the field. Go over another stile in the corner – take care, as you emerge on to a lane.

Q: What is the strange sounding name of the house on the right?

4.  Walk down the lane to the right, round the bend. Ignore the footpath on the opposite side of the road. Continue down the hill and turn right on to a track/driveway.

☺ Can you see the half-hidden footpath sign?

5.  On the left is a yellow footpath arrow, take this narrow path into the woods, passing a house and garden on the left. Take care – narrow path – single file.

6.  The path rejoins the track and continues straight. It then goes

down three steps on the left and then right down some stone steps. Follow the path down, then up to emerge alongside a private house and garden.

7.   Go past the house and back into the woods through a gate.

☺ In summer, look for butterflies on the buddleia across the path. You are most likely to see Painted Ladies, Small Tortoiseshells, Red Admirals and Gatekeepers. They are attracted to flowers and found in most places. Painted Ladies are the world's most common butterfly. Red Admirals can fly at speeds of 25km per hour.

Painted Lady

8.   Follow the path through the woods.

☺ Use your tracking skills along this path. Look for the yellow arrows painted on the trees.

9.   The narrow path widens into a shady, pine needle-strewn path through tall trees.

☺ To the right is the site of a motte which is a similar earth structure to the Iron Age forts, but not as old.

10.  Follow the path round twists and turns to a stile. To the left is a small, open field.

11.  Follow the path alongside a shallow stream.

☺ Look for frogs and sticklebacks. There are 3400 species of frogs and toads. They are amphibians and so live mainly on the land but breed in water. The common frog is grey or brown or yellow with blotches and will be found in damp vegetation. Frogs cannot crawl on land, they hop or leap. Sticklebacks are named after the spines on their backs which may be for protection against enemies. The male is the more devoted parent!

**Common Frog**

12. **The path then bends away from the stream to a stile. Go over the stile and turn left.**

☺ Look for pheasants and butterflies clustered around puddles in the summer.

13. **Go through a gate and follow the track uphill. Then leave the track so as to continue straight to a stile next to a drystone wall.**

☺ Make sure you're in front to be the first across the next bit!

14. **Go over a stile then follow the path across to another stile, across a bridge, down some steps and across the stepping stones. Follow the path up to a stile.**

☺ On the right is a big pond which is likely to have lots of ducks on it.

15. **Turn left then cross the grass to join the higher track and go**

right slightly uphill, following blue and yellow arrows and horse signs.

16. The path climbs uphill, round a bend and through a gateway. Go past a house on the right and continue straight along the driveway of the house and through a farmyard.

☺ Look over to the right, on the far hill is the church you saw at the beginning. It is partially hidden by trees, but can you see the gravestones?

17. Continue along the lane away from the farm. The lane emerges on to the main road through Brimpsfield. Turn right and walk through the village to your car.

Q: Can you find The Old Post Office and the Old Forge? Do you know what a forge is?

A: A forge is where blacksmiths make horseshoes and other metal objects.

# *The Long Barrows Walk*

The two long barrows that are on the route are excellent examples of Stone Age man's burial chambers. The Nympsfield Long Barrow, at the starting point, is open air. The Uley Long Barrow still has an intact roof. So take a torch and climb in. The starting point of the walk, Coaley Peak, is a popular place at all times of the year. In the winter you can enjoy a bracing wind as you stand and look out over 'the whole world', then walk into the shelter of the woods. In the spring and summer there are kite fliers, and gliders and hang-gliders fill the skies. Now the woods provide some welcome shade. The beautiful views make this a wonderful place to stand and stare, or walk and wonder.

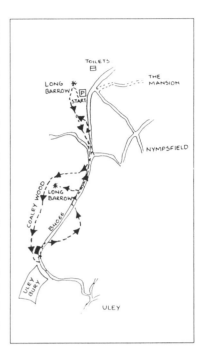

| | |
|---|---|
| **Starting point:** | Head south on the A38 out of Gloucester. Take the turn off to Frocester, up Frocester Hill to join the B4066. Turn left to find the car park, signposted Nympsfield Long Barrow. |
| **Distance:** | 3 miles |
| **Terrain:** | Some narrow, steep paths, but mostly wide and wooded. Some mud where bridleways cross. There is a short distance that has to be walked on the verge of the road, but it is wide enough. |
| **Map:** | O.S. Landranger 162 |
| **Public Toilets:** | Car park |
| **Refreshments:** | Ice cream van in the car park, picnic area |
| **Pushchairs:** | Not really suitable for pushchairs |

1.  **From the car park, the Nympsfield Long Barrow is straight up from the entrance to the car park.**

☺ In the spring look for cowslips.

The Long Barrow has an information board in front of it.

2.  **From the Long Barrow, walk back past the car park to look out over the Severn Vale.**

☺ Now you can see for miles and miles, all the way to Wales.

The River Severn is a shining strip of silver in the distance, and the fields and houses before look like models. You are 800 feet (250 metres) above sea level. An information board tells you what you can see across the Vale. Can you point out May Hill?

Q: What apparently tiny animals can you see in the fields below?

3.  **Continue on, to the gate in the far corner, on the edge of the hill. The National Trust sign for Coaley Peak has an information board by it.**

4.  **Go through the gate and turn left down a short, steep bank. Then walk along a wide, grassy path at the edge of the hill. At the fork, take the path on the right which is quite narrow at first.**

☺ See the disused quarry to the left where Cotswold stone was cut to build houses, walls, fireplaces and many other things.

5.  **The path continues through what looks like a jungle ravine with high sides and lush undergrowth. There are three small steps cut into the path.**

☺ Look out for rare orchids. Are the large black birds nesting amongst the rocks crows, rooks or ravens?

The raven is the largest member of the crow family and possibly the most intelligent of birds. The raven is bigger than the crow with a thicker beak and shaggy throat feathers. Listen for its strange duck-like honking call. The crow is a very territorial bird, and very aggressive. It will drive off birds of prey and even foxes. Listen for its familiar caw sound.

Left to right: crow, rook and raven

6. **Pass a rockfall warning sign and keep straight on at the next path fork. Up ahead are some steep steps. At the top is the road, so take care on emerging.**

☺ See the large fissure in the rock face. Do not climb the rocks as that may cause the rocks to fall, but it is safe to pass by.

7. **Cross the road to walk facing the traffic. It is only a short stretch along the road. Pass the milestone at the top and go straight on to the Cotswold Way sign.**

☺ Milestones told riders and carriage drivers the distance and the way to towns in the days before cars and modern road signs.

8. **Follow the sign and enter the woods. It is a quite steep downhill path, but not too difficult for little legs.**

☺ In spring look out for wood anemones and primroses.

9. **At a small fork in the path, go right, but at the bigger fork go left and begin to climb. Fork left again up to a gate with an arrow.**

☺ Look out as you emerge from the woods into the open and see the view to your right. If you face out, Cam Long Down is the strange-shaped hill to the left which you will also have seen from a different angle back at the viewpoint near the car park.

10. **Follow the level, narrow path, then go up a short, steep climb.**

☺ Spooky cave to the left. Intrepid explorers can make their way across the stones to have a look but it is advisable not to climb in. In spring look for forget-me-nots by the path.

11. **Continue along the path, which is now quite wide. Go through a gate and up to Cotswold Way signs and a parking area.**

    If you wish to add an extra mile on to the walk, you could walk around Uley Bury, an Iron Age fort. Go out on to the road and follow the Cotswold Way signs to the right.

12. **Cross the road to walk along the verge to the left. Just past the houses on the left, the path bends right, away from the road, past a Fire Danger sign.**

Q: What are the long-handled rubber shovels used for that are leaning against the Fire Danger sign?

13. **Pass through a broken gate leading into a field. Take the right-hand path through the woods. At a fork stay left to remain parallel to the field. The path curves to the left around the field.**

14. **The path then opens out and gently climbs to the left back to the road (B4066). Cross the road to the verge and turn right. Walk to the brown sign directing you to Uley Long Barrow. Follow this across the field.**

☺ This Long Barrow is also known as Hetty Pegler's Tump. It still has its roof on so you can crawl through the doorway and have a look. It is very small inside, not like a cave but like a tiny room. There are three small chambers leading off. This is where the bodies would have been put. It is very dark inside so take a torch.

15. **Walk back to the road and continue along the verge to the left. It is quite wide but look out for drainage ditches.**

☺ Past the new road sign are two old milestones.

Q: Can you read the name on the second milestone?

16. **Continue past the entrance to the woods which was used in Direction 8. Cross the road and follow the left-hand verge. The verge is wide and the road is quieter along here. Follow the path along the fence and go through the gate straight in front, back on to Coaley Peak. The car park is straight ahead.**

☺ There is usually an ice cream van in the car park!

### Other Attractions

If you go out of the car park and turn left on to the B4066, a hundred yards up the road, on the right, are some old gates. This is the entrance to Woodchester Mansion. The house was abandoned half-way through building, in 1890, because the owner ran out of money. It is a fascinating look at a would-be stately home. Like a ghost house, it is as if the stonemasons left only yesterday. There are no floors or ceilings, but intricate stone carving and fireplaces that seem to hang in mid-air. Older children will enjoy the half-finished mystery, but younger children will need to be watched up and down the stone

steps and across uneven dirt floors. They can't make a mess
though!The mansion is at the end of a lovely mile walk down into
the valley. It is open on the first weekend of every month from Easter
to October and Bank Holidays, too. There is an admission charge
and dogs are not allowed into the valley. Guided tours are led by the
Friends when a queue forms.

# *Walk Like a Roman – Chedworth Woods*

This is a beautiful woodland walk with the trees, flowers and wildlife serving as the main attraction. However, the walk starts, and ends, at the Roman villa. This is well worth a visit for its stunning mosaic floors, though there is an admission charge. The setting is beautiful, it's so peaceful, as if you really have gone back in time. Linger in the lush valley and wander through the surrounding woods and fields. A perfect day out.

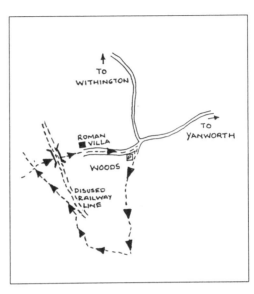

---

**Starting point:**  Chedworth Roman Villa. The villa is conveniently situated within reach of three major roads, depending on which direction you are coming from – the A436, the A40 and the A429. The nearest villages are Withington and Compton Abdale. The villa is well signed. The Woodland Car Park is on the left just before the villa itself.

**Distance:**  2 miles

**Terrain:**  Woodland and field paths, shared bridle paths could be muddy after rain.

**Map:**  O.S. Landranger 163

**Public Toilets:**  There are toilets at the villa.

**Refreshments:**  Ice cream and sweets for sale at the villa. Pub in the village of Withington.

**Pushchairs:**  Roots across and stones on paths may make it difficult.

---

1.  **Walk back out of the Woodland Car Park, turn left and then right over the stile next to a gate.**

☺ This is a game and wildlife conservation area so look out for birds and butterflies. We saw lots of tiny brown butterflies, called Ringlets (June). Ringlets are dark brown to black in colour with dim eyespots on both wings. They are commonly seen in woodland.

**Ringlet butterfly**

2.  **Follow the path into the woods.**

☺ Look out for footpath signs and arrows.

3.  **The path gradually climbs uphill.**

☺ On the left is the large stump of a dead tree. Its outstretched limbs make it look like a totem pole.

4.  **Pass through an old gateway at the top of the climb.**

☺ Look at the moss-covered drystone wall. Moss was the first type of plant to take over the land, nearly 400 million years ago.

5.  **The path curves to the right and you pass a bridleway sign.**

☺ Listen! What can you hear?

6.  **Go through an old gateway with a broken gate propped up alongside.**

☺ See how the tree roots make steps across the path.

7. The path emerges alongside fields and widens into a track.

8. Turn right at the end, following blue bridle path signs but also signs to the Roman Villa.

☺ As you walk, look at the drystone wall alongside to your left. How long do you think it would have taken to build? How many stones would be needed? Look across the fields. Can you see any more of these walls?

9. Go through a gate at the end and turn right along the field.

Q: What is growing in this field?

10. At the bottom of the field is a wide stile taking you back into the woods. There is a short, steep downhill section then a long, wide track through the woods.

☺ Partly hidden in the undergrowth is a sign pointing to the Roman Villa. Can you find it? Look carefully to the right.

11. Keep straight when the path also leads to the left. Another short, steep downhill section. At the bottom is a multi-arrowed post at a path crossroads. Turn right.

☺ Look for another hidden Roman Villa sign.

12. The path is downhill and quite uneven. Take care. Go under the old railway bridge.

☺ Don't forget to make some echoes! Just after the bridge, on the right, are some steps leading up to the disused railway track above. If you are feeling energetic, and this is the end of the walk, they are good fun to run up. Walk to the right and you are on the bridge you have just walked under. The Cheltenham to Cirencester railway line closed in 1961.

13. Go back down to the path and follow it along to its end, at the Roman Villa.

14. To return to the car park, follow the road away from the villa and go up some steps on the right.

# The Weir Walk – Maisemore

This is a beautiful walk for a summer's day, with an abundance of wild flowers and butterflies along the path. The route follows the River Severn past the crashing, swirling weir and then climbs Spring Hill to more wonderful views of Gloucestershire. Feel free to burst into a few verses of *The Hills Are Alive*!

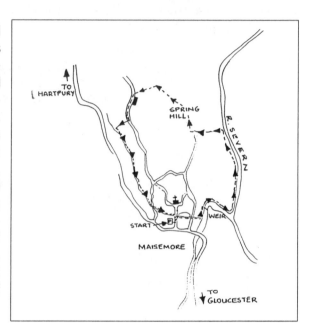

**Starting point:**  Maisemore Village Hall, off Church Road in the village of Maisemore which can be found on the A417, to the west of Gloucester. Church Road is on the right.

**Distance:**  4 miles

**Terrain:**  Grassy tracks and field paths. One short steep hill and also a short distance along a country lane.

**Map:**  O.S. Landranger 162

**Toilets:**  No

**Refreshments:**  Two public houses in Maisemore village

**Pushchairs:**  Yes, wide enough paths, but you must be prepared to carry it up and down three lots of steps and over a few stiles.

1. **From the car park at the village hall, turn left down Church Road, walking towards the church.**

☺ Look for wild flowers in the hedgerows. We saw vetch, buttercups, cow parsley and speedwell in June.

2. **Turn right along the signed footpath past a large lake.**

☺ Look out for ducks and geese, and their babies at the right time of year. Also yellow water irises. There are islands in the middle of the lake. In September you might find this a good spot for blackberries.

The Canada goose, with its long black neck and white chin strap is the largest European goose. Originally from Canada, it can now be found in many parts of Europe, most of America and even New Zealand. Flocks fly in V formations and adults mate for life. The male and female look alike. Ducks are found on all inland waters, at coasts and estuaries. The common mallard has a distinctive bottle green head. Only ducks (females) quack, drakes (males) grunt and whistle.

Yellow Iris

3. **At the end of the lake, go down a narrow flight of steps on the right and across a small bridge. Just beyond the bridge is a lane so take care on emerging.**

4. **Turn left down the lane, cross over and go over the stile on the right, along the Severn Way path. Walk straight along the bottom of the field. When we walked through in early June, it was a pea field.**

☺ Adventurous explorers can run along paths that dip down to the right, down to a small stream, without losing sight of the main path.

**5.   The path bends to the left, following the course of the river.**

☺ Can you hear that crashing sound? What on earth can it be? Who can be the first to see the weir through gaps in the bushes?

**6.   At the stile there is a good view of the weir. Walk across the field to a stile on the right.**

☺ For a really good view of the weir make your way carefully through the trees just before the stile and look through the fence at the foaming water. A weir is a man-made construction to control the flow of water.

**7.   Cross the stile and follow the path over a small floodgate. The path continues straight. Pass a horse jump on your left.**

☺ Notice how the noise of the weir is gradually dying away. Look through the trees to the river at the bend.

Q:  Can you see a road sign which refers to boats? What does it say?

**8.   The path bends to the left with the river.**

☺ Look out over the trees on the hill across the field. Can you see a big white house? Who might live in such a beautiful house? Look out for a variety of butterflies.

**9.   Continue along the path, over a stile and across the next field.**

☺ You can wave at boats as they pass and even to the walkers on the path on the other side of the river. See the markers in the trees to measure the water height. Riverbanks should have plenty of wildlife. Look for dippers, kingfishers, damselflies and water voles. Otters signal a healthy river.

10. When you reach a hedgerow turn left, walking away from the river.

☺ See the prehistoric-looking wild rhubarb with its giant leaves. (June)

11. At the end of the field go through the tall wooden gate on the right and climb the hill.

☺ It is a steep climb but you can see the post with the arrow on which marks the top, so the end is always in sight! Once up, it is worth the view. You are so high that birds seem to fly below you.

Q: Can you see Gloucester Cathedral?

12. Walk along the top of the hill to the gate. There is another gate immediately after. Pass through both. Walk straight on, keeping the fence and the view on your right. It's quite a long, steady climb along the edge of the field.

☺ Look down at the lake below. You may even see a heron flying over from the river. There is a lot to see and everything looks so small, the houses, sheep and trees. Far away you can see the river with tiny boats on it.

13. At the top of the field follow the arrow to the left. At the end is another arrow as the path emerges on to a lane. Turn left and follow the lane past houses and farms.

☺ On the left, and then on the right, is an 'apiary' or bee farm. Can you see the hives? Honey bees were originally a tropical insect but can now be found everywhere. The queen bee spends most of her time laying eggs. When a honey bee finds a good source of food it does a dance in a figure of eight pattern to show other bees where it is.

14. The road bends slightly uphill and the footpath is on the right. There is a sign by a tree to look out for. Walk straight across towards the line of trees. The cars on the A417 can be seen in front.

☺ You can see the city of Gloucester over to the left.

15. **At the edge of the field turn left, following the line of trees by the side of a small stream. Continue on into the next field.**

☺ Look out for the top of Maisemore Church tower. Now you know you are nearly back at the car!

16. **Take some intrepid steps through the hedge down on to the lane.**

☺ These steps are quite steep and overgrown and some steps are missing so small children might need help. An adult should go first as the steps emerge on to the lane.

17. **Cross the lane and go up the steps opposite. Go over a stile and into a field. Keep straight ahead.**

☺ Round the bend and you will see the back of the village hall, keep going.

18. **The path emerges on to a lane opposite the path taken in point 2. Turn right, and right again for the car park.**

# '*Do it in stile*' – *Ashleworth Tithe Barn*

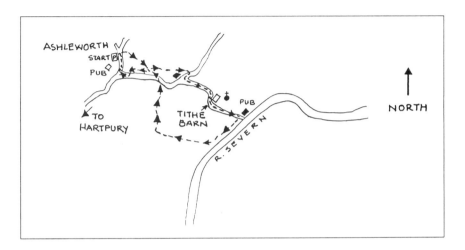

This walk is all on the flat and quite short, but with lots of stiles and likely to be very muddy during the wetter months. The 15th-century tithe barn that you pass along the way is 120 feet (37 metres) long and belongs to the National Trust. Past the barn is the River Severn and a lovely spot for a rest, complete with a tiny inn on the bank. But if your children are anything like ours, then the main attraction will be the many stiles to hunt down along the route, 15 in all!

| | |
|---|---|
| **Starting point:** | Ashleworth village, which is off the A417, north of Gloucester. Turn right at Hartpury. Park on the road through the village, just past the village green, next to The Queen's Arms. |
| **Distance:** | 2½ miles |
| **Terrain:** | Flat, field tracks, very muddy after rain. |
| **Map:** | O.S. Landranger 162 |
| **Refreshments:** | Two public houses with gardens, The Queen's Arms in the village and The Boat Inn by the river. |

1.  The footpath is on the right, just past The Queen's Arms. Start over a stile and go past a garden to another stile.

☺ Peek quietly over the fence into the garden to see the birds in the aviary.

2.  Walk across the field to a stile at the bottom right of the field, though not to the furthest stile.

☺ Look for yellow arrows.

**Snow Goose**

3.  Go straight across the field to the next stile.

☺ If you stand on the stile for a moment and look across the fields ahead, you can see the church and the barn.

4.  Walk across the field to the road. Turn right along the road, then left at the old-fashioned signpost, towards the Quay.

Q: What other places does the signpost point to?

5.  Follow the lane to the church and tithe barn. Pass a graveyard on the left and then a flood depth gauge. The tithe barn is in front of you.

☺ "Tithe" was the proportion, one tenth, of a villager's produce etc. that had to be given to the church.

6.  Continue down the lane.

☺ Look for ducks and geese around the farmyard. Ducks are very common on all inland waters. They were among the first birds to be domesticated 4500 years ago. The males usually have more colourful feathers than the females. Some ducks up-end and feed in shallow water, other ducks dive deep. Geese live mainly on the land and feed on grasses.

7. **Go through a black metal floodgate and past a house to the river. The Boat Inn is on the left and the quay straight ahead.**

☺ Look for the old advert signs. Modern advertising began 150 years ago when factories first produced goods in large quantities.

8. **Turn right over a stile, past a floodgate and over two mores stiles. Then walk straight along the edge of the field alongside the river.**

☺ River banks provide good homes for many types of wildlife – dippers, kingfishers, damselflies and water voles. Otters signal a healthy river.

9. **About halfway along is a path going straight across the field. It is marked by a post indicating Permissive Path (Bridle Path).**

☺ Scout ahead to find the path across the field.

10. **Go across the field and over a ditch into the next field. Continue straight across to the hedge and a stile in the corner.**

☺ Look out for horses.

11. **This bit is tricky. Bear left across the field, the stile is not in sight until you are quite a way across, then it is in front of you, tucked in a corner.**

12. **Go straight ahead to another stile, then to a second and then a third. This final one emerges on to the road so take care.**

13. Turn left and cross to a kissing gate and a footpath on the right. Follow the path across the field to a stile.

14. Go straight, through a gateway with a yellow-arrowed post, and then straight up to the left-hand corner of the field and a stile next to a black and white timbered house.

15. Go down steps to the lane and turn right up the lane. Pass the village school and the village green with its old stone memorial. Turn right at the top for the pub and starting point.

# *Along the Gloucester and Sharpness Canal – Frampton on Severn*

Frampton is a pretty village, famed for having the largest village green in Gloucestershire. The canal runs alongside the village and the walk follows the towpath between Splatt Bridge and Frampton Bridge. The entire canal is 16 miles long and 30 metres wide. When it was opened in 1827 it was the largest in the country. Canals were an ideal alternative to a bumpy, old road and a horse and cart for transporting goods around the country. They could carry more and were smoother and quicker. At the bridges, note the style of the bridge keepers' cottages, with their Greek style Doric columns. Across from

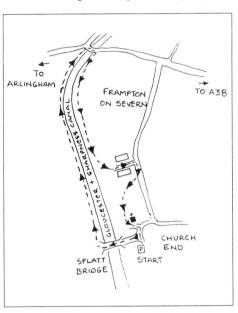

the canal is the river Severn and between the two are some flooded gravel pits which should provide you with plenty of bird sightings. At the end of the walk is the church, which is worth the detour to feel the front door. Apparently, it is covered with a wild boar skin from the time when wild boar roamed this area.

---

| | |
|---|---|
| **Starting point:** | Frampton is off the A38 to the south of Gloucester. Drive through the village green, past the church to a public car park just before Splatt Bridge. |
| **Distance:** | 2 miles |
| **Map:** | Landranger 162 |
| **Terrain:** | Very flat, towpath and field paths, will be muddy after rain. |
| **Refreshments:** | Two pubs and some shops in the village. |

---

1.  **Leave the car park, turn left and walk over Splatt Bridge.**

☺ If you are lucky and a boat is coming, then you will be able to see how the bridge is opened to let boats through.

2.  **Turn right and walk along the towpath.**

☺ See the church over to your right and the river Severn to your left. Look for swans, moorhens, gulls, ducks and maybe even a heron. Swans are the largest of waterfowl, they can be quite vicious so approach with caution. If you see a large grey one, then it is still a baby even if it is as big as its parents. Mute swans are very common, they can be identified by their orange bills with the black knob. Swans form partnerships for life.

3.  **Round the curve of the canal and the next bridge comes into sight.**

☺ Look out for brightly-painted canal boats.

4.  **Cross the bridge and turn right to walk a short way along the opposite side of the canal.**

5.  **Go over a stile and turn left. Turn right at the post with the two yellow arrows so that you follow a field path parallel with the canal.**

6.  **The path curves round away from the canal and then right into some trees and hedges. There is a post with a yellow arrow on it to mark the way. Follow this narrow path to a short, steep bank to your left and a stile on the right.**

7.  **Go over the stile and walk diagonally across the field to the corner past the wall where there is a track leading to a stile. You cannot see this exit until you are a good way across the field, but if you just head towards the houses you should find it.**

Q: Do you know what creature makes the small mounds of earth which are all over this field?

A: Moles. They can lift 20 times their own weight of soil with their powerful front claws. They are blind and deaf so use vibrations through their sensitive snouts to find food, usually worms.

**8. Go over the stile and down the lane. Turn right at the end. Pass a red telephone box.**

Q: What is on the weather vane on top of Narles House? (the house opposite the phone box, on your right.)

**9. Go through the gate and along the avenue of trees to the church.**

Q: What type of tree makes the avenue?

A: Horse chestnut. Look out for the fallen one. Horse chestnut trees have leaves like hands. The 'horse' part of the name comes from the Turks who used parts of the tree to treat their horses.

**10. The entrance to the church is through a metal kissing gate, just past the trees. Walk round to the front of the church.**

☺ Feel the church door. What does it feel like? Does it feel like wood? Or something else? It is covered with wild boar skin.

**Wild boar**

Wild boars became extinct in Britain in the 17th century but they still exist in other parts of the world. They are the ancestors of our domestic pig. They have sharp tusks and are quite dangerous. The wild boar does not have a curly tail like a farm pig, it has a straight one so it can swat at flies.

11. **Go out of the churchyard, through the gate with the lamp above it and turn right. Go through the wooden gate and turn left. Walk across the field to a stile opposite the car park.**

For more information on canals, The National Waterways Museum at Gloucester Docks, Gloucester, is the place to go. It is open every day, 10am to 5pm during the winter, and until 6pm in the summer. The admission price is quite high but it is well worth a visit and has many interesting displays.

## Other Attractions

Just down the road from Frampton is St. Augustine's Farm at Arlingham which is a working farm and has pigs, sheep, ducks, chickens, horses and a room full of rabbits! Open March-Sept. Admission charge.

# ℐ 𝒲atery 𝒲alk from 𝒰pper to ℒower 𝒮laughter

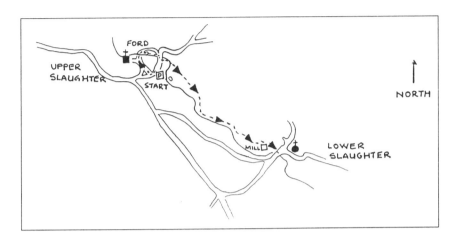

This is a short, simple walk from Upper to Lower Slaughter and then back again along the same path. Children should enjoy the confidence of knowing the route on the way back. There are a number of kissing gates to pass through, and ducks on the mill pond at Lower Slaughter so take some bread. Also at Lower Slaughter are the mill shop and Mill Museum, housed in the old water mill. Refreshments and crafts are for sale. Wear your wellies and wade in the ford at Upper Slaughter, or dare to bare your toes in the summer! Thanks to the Simms family for suggesting this walk and coming with us.

| | |
|---|---|
| **Starting point:** | Upper Slaughter village, off the A429 near Bourton on the Water. Park along the road outside the Lord of the Manor Hotel and Restaurant, or in the village square. |
| **Distance:** | 2 miles |
| **Map:** | O.S. Landranger 163 |
| **Refreshments:** | Mill shop, Lower Slaughter |
| **Pushchairs:** | Yes, if you can negotiate the gates |

1. **Walk up the lane away from the Lord of the Manor, back into the village. From the village square follow signs to the ford.**

☺ If you've got your wellies on, have a wade!

2. **Next to the ford, on the small bridge, is a stile. Cross this stile and follow the path alongside the stream. At the end is a giant stile!**

3. **Turn right up the lane. On the left is a footpath marked Warden's Way.**

☺ A bridge crosses the fast-flowing stream, which may be good for Pooh sticks. Try dropping a stick in and seeing if it comes through.

4. **Go over the bridge and through a gate. Follow the path across the field.**

☺ See a pond over to your right.

5. **Through another kissing gate and straight across the field to another kissing gate.**

6. **Continue straight across to another kissing gate, and now the path runs alongside the River Eye.**

☺ Look out for the floodgate about halfway along.

7. **Go through a kissing gate with a small plaque on it.**

Q: Whose wedding does the plaque commemorate?

8. **You are now in Lower Slaughter. Turn right for the mill, with its shop, museum and waterwheel.**

☺ Look for the ducks on the Mill pond, and the waterwheel over to the right.

Q: What did the wheel do?

A: It powered the machinery that ground the flour, as this was a flour mill.

Mallards: duck and drake

Ducks are common to all inland waters, at coasts and estuaries. You can easily spot the most common, the mallard, as the male has a distinctive bottle green head. Only ducks (females) quack, drakes (males) whistle and grunt.

9. Follow the narrow path alongside the water into the village. It is a pretty village with lots of water and bridges. When you have finished looking around, retrace your steps back to Upper Slaughter.

10. When you reach the Warden's Way sign at the beginning of the footpath in Upper Slaughter, turn left and walk up the lane into the village to your starting point.

## Other Attractions

Nearby, off the A429, is Bourton on the Water which has lots to offer a visitor. a model village, a museum, the Bird Garden and a perfumery. Follow the appropriate brown signs from the main road.

If you want to see some more ducks, other waterfowl and poultry, go to Folly Farm off the A436 towards Cheltenham. Again, follow the brown signs with the duck on them. Admission charge.

# ℐ *Walk on the Cloud* – *Cleeve Hill*

This area is a popular spot for walkers and so there are many paths, though some, confusingly, are sheep trails. Our route takes you along the low road up the hill, and back along the high road. The views are fantastic and the terrain is interesting, formed as a result of quarrying for limestone over the centuries. Younger children will enjoy the close proximity to lots of sheep and older children can play at being a close relative to the

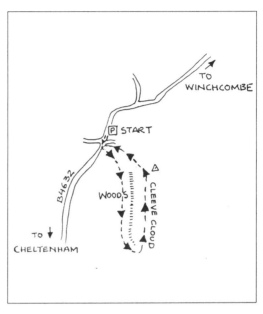

sheep, the mountain goat, without having to venture far from the path. Adults can enjoy the invigorating air and the amazing view.

---

**Starting point:** Cleeve Hill. Parking is available near the top of the hill which can be found on the Winchcombe Road, the B4632, out of Cheltenham.

**Distance:** 2½ miles

**Terrain:** Grassy tracks, some steep bits

**Map:** O.S. Landranger 163

**Toilets:** At the parking area

**Refreshments:** Possibly an ice cream van at the parking area, and a pub with a garden back down the hill.

**Pushchairs:** Possibly suitable for a rugged, travel-buggy type.

---

1. **Go back down the hill, past the toilets to a gate and stile on the left, opposite Stockwell Lane.**

☺ As you climb over the stile, opposite you is a large board with the Bylaws of the Common written on it. Bylaws can be quite interesting, you may find that you can do things you would not expect, like graze your pigs or forage for firewood. You can also find out what you cannot do!

2. **Follow the track to the right on the easiest path to follow, keeping parallel to the hill. Pass some houses on the right.**

☺ Look out for sheep. Sheep were first domesticated 10 000 years ago and today there are 800 varieties. Their thick, warm wool is very valuable to humans.

3. **At the footpath signs at the end of the path, go straight past the 'no cars, no motorbikes' road signs. It is now a steady climb up to an uneven road.**

☺ Keep checking over your shoulder at the view. But also look up to your left and see if there are any rock climbers.

4. **Climb on up to the shade of a small copse on the right.**

Q: What type of trees are in the copse?
A: Beech. The beech tree can support 200 species of invertebrate e.g. slugs, centipedes and wood lice.

5. **Continue along the road. At a fork go left past a huge boulder practically blocking the path.**

☺ Look out for birds of prey, hares and grasshoppers. The birds of prey you are most likely to see are sparrow hawks, buzzards and kestrels (they're the ones you often see hovering by the sides of motorways). Birds of prey hunt other animals, catching them alive. True birds of prey have sharp talons and hooked beaks. They are well known for their superb eyesight. See them soar in the air, hover, then drop on to their prey.

6. At a grass plateau with a bench, turn to the right and follow the narrow path down to the wider one. Follow this path around the edge of the hill and then up on to it. At the top, turn left, through a tree archway, and out towards the edge of the hill. Turn right and walk, carefully, along the edge.

☺ Can you see the racecourse? Also look out for rabbit holes, and golfers!

**Brown Hare**

7. Follow the path towards the post at the top.

☺ This post is a triangulation point and is used for map-making.

8. Carry on to the next post with an arrow on it. Continue past the point where the rock climbers climb to. Keep to the outer path.

9. Continue straight all the way over many undulations and follow the path through a small gully. Start dropping down to the starting point when the house with the walled garden, and the Bylaws board, come into view. Go back over the stile that you entered over. Take care as you emerge on to the road.

# *Down in the Valley – Toadsmoor Valley*

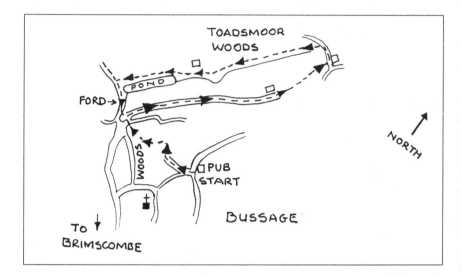

This walk was suggested to us by the novelist Jilly Cooper for its abundance of beautiful wild flowers in the spring and summer. We walked it in the autumn so the flowers were gone. The beauty of the walk was not diminished by the lack of flowers, but further enhanced by the amazing golds, greens, russets and reds of the leaves on the varieties of trees. Near the end of the walk is Toadsmoor Lake, a large and serene body of water, hidden in the valley. And round the corner is a ford, so wear your wellies and wade!

---

**Starting point:**   Bussage village, which can be found off the A418 between Stroud and Cirencester. Park in the village, opposite The Ram public house.

**Distance:**   2 miles

**Map:**   O.S. Landranger 162

**Terrain:**   Open tracks and woodland paths

**Refreshments:**   The Ram, Bussage

---

1. Follow the sign to the church down the lane immediately opposite the pub, marked as unsuitable for motors. Go past some pretty stone houses and turn right on to the public footpath and over a stile.

2. Follow the path up to another stile, then straight across the top of the field to a hedgerow. Turn left on the other side of the hedgerow and go down the hill to the stile.

3. Go over this stile and follow the path, right, through the woods.

☺ There is a stone stile at the bottom of this path, but take care on emerging as the road is on the other side, though there is a wide verge.

4. Go down some steps to the road and cross over. Follow the right-hand track.

Q: What is the name of the cottage opposite where you emerged from the woods? And when was it built?

5. Continue along this track, through a gateway.

☺ Look out for the lake down to the left and look at the shapes and colours of the trees rising up from it.

6. The track seems to fork, but the left-hand track is just for access to a building so continue straight ahead.

☺ Look for blackberries in autumn. Also look out for a small, fancy iron gate, and then look through the trees to a house in the woods.

7. Continue straight, and after a while the track begins to climb. Pass a house on the right. Go through a gateway.

8. Continue straight to a black gate and a stile next to a house. Go down the track and through a wooden gateway. At a metal gate, go over the stile and turn left down the lane.

☺ The cottage opposite the metal gate and stile looks like

something out of a fairy tale. Hansel and Gretel, perhaps? Snow White? What do you think?

9.  **Cross a bridge into the woods.**

☺ If you look carefully over the metal fence of the bridge, there is a steep drop below you.

10. **Turn sharp left into the woods, and go down alongside a tiny stream. Follow the path all the way.**

11. **Eventually a garden opens out to your left and there is a house on the right.**

Q: Who lived, or lives, in this house? (Clue – see the name of it to find out.)

12. **Follow the path straight on until you are walking alongside the water.**

☺ Look for ducks, and fish popping up to the surface to feed. You may even see a heron (we did) but you have to be quiet as they are very nervous of people. There are some stone steps leading down to the water so you can get closer if you want but take care of the edge. The steps are nice to sit on and just look for a little while, to see what you can see.

Grey herons are the most common and largest of European herons, but are sometimes difficult to spot as they can stand so motionless in the water. At nearly a metre high, the heron is Britain's tallest bird. Look at the picture opposite! They are a majestic sight, especially in the air.

The Moorhen is a small, black, duck-like bird with a distinctive red beak. They are a very successful species, found everywhere, and this is partly due to the fact that they will eat almost anything. Plants, berries, seeds, insects, worms, slugs and even the young, and eggs, of other bird species.

13. At the end of the track turn left. Follow the track up and over a bridge.

☺ Or go through the ford if you have your wellies on!

14. On the left, just before a house, is a steep, narrow path going back up to the road. Go up here and retrace steps 4, 3, 2 and 1 back to the car.

**Heron**

# A Farm Walk to the Hangman's Stone – Yanworth

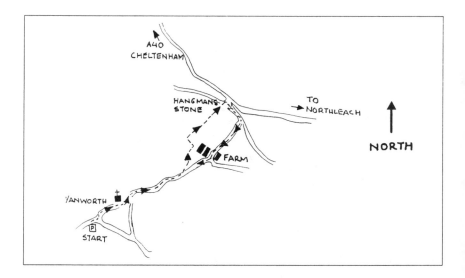

This walk takes in plenty of the beautiful Gloucestershire countryside, mainly rolling farm land around the pretty village of Yanworth. The Church is Norman in parts, 12th century in others, with medieval glass. Note the similarity of style to the Church at Brimpsfield. The Hangman's Stone either marks the site of a gibbet, or has taken its name from an incident with a sheep rustler climbing over and becoming entangled with sheep, rope and stone, and so hanging himself. Others speculate that it is a Bronze Age monolith. When you have found it, and it is half-hidden and probably wholly ignored, decide for yourself and make up your own story. A short section of the walk is along the road known as Salt Way. This is so named because in medieval times the road was principally developed as a means of transporting salt, a very important commodity in medieval times. The road eventually links up with the Thames at Lechlade. One more thing, when we did this walk we saw a deer bound down the track near the Hangman's Stone and then quickly disappear into a small copse. So keep your eyes peeled!

**Starting point:** Yanworth village. Take the A40 out of Cheltenham towards Oxford. Turn right after the Puesdown Inn (now called The Cotswold Explorer). Go past signs to Compton Abdale, turn right, then right again at a crossroads. Follow signs to Yanworth. Park on the road opposite a row of cottages with green doors.

**Distance:** 3 miles

**Terrain:** Farm roads and lanes, fields and a short section along a quiet road with verge (Salt Way).

**Map:** O.S. Landranger 163

**Pushchairs:** Ninety per cent is suitable for pushchairs (see point 3).

1. **Walk back past the row of cottages to the corner house and turn left up the lane, then right along a quiet lane. Go past a row of houses on the left. At the bottom is a farm and the church.**

☺ Have a quick, quiet look inside the church

2. **Go through the farmyard to the left and continue along the lane which bears to the right.**

☺ This is a game and wildlife conservation area so see what you can see. Look also for farm animals.

3. **The lane goes steadily downhill, then steeply uphill with a sharp bend to the right, and then round to the left at the top. Walk along the level section and on the left is a gate with a yellow footpath arrow on it. Go through the gate and follow the path.**

This is the bit that may be difficult for pushchairs.

4. **Go over a stile and follow a fenced-in path next to a drystone wall.**

☺ Look down to the left for super farmland views. In the spring a plough breaks the soil for planting, a seed drill plants the seed and covers it up. Later, a sprayer kills off harmful diseases and pests and then the combine harvester cuts the crop and prepares it for storage in late summer. Depending on what time of year you walk, you will see one of these stages or will be able to tell which has just been done. Which is it?

5. **Go over the gate at the end and climb up on to concrete. Turn left and walk straight down through the gateway at the bottom. Turn right and walk along edge of the field.**

6. **Continue up (it is a steady climb), under the electricity lines and past the pylon. Go through a gateway.**

☺ On the right is the Hangman's Stone. Can you find it? It is lying on its side against the wall, hidden in the undergrowth. It is difficult to see the shape of it, but it has a hole at the top and looks a bit like a key.

7. **Turn right along the track, which then emerges on to the lane, Salt Way. Turn right and walk along the road/verge. Up ahead is a white signpost and footpath sign which indicates how far you will have to walk along the road.**

8. **Turn right along the road to the farm.**

☺ Look out for tractors.

9. **Walk through the farm. Follow the track to the left, then turn right.**

☺ Look for cows in the barn, sheep dogs, old stone steps over a wall, straw bales, a combine harvester, a cattle grid and triangle-shaped windows in the stone barn. People have been keeping animals on farms for 9000 years, after domesticating wild animals. Farms produce meat, eggs, milk, butter, cheese, wool and leather. In the 18th century there was an agricultural revolution, and vast changes were made – new methods, new crops, new machines and improved breeding.

**10. Turn right again and then left.**

☺ Look for footprints in the cement, tyres, feed sacks, log piles and wool sacks. Anything else?

**11. Pass through a gateway and down the lane away from the farm. Pass the gate in point 3.**

**12. Retrace steps of points 3, 2 and 1 back down the lane, through the farmyard, past the church and up to Yanworth and the car.**

☺ Were you lucky enough to see a deer, too?

The deer was probably a red deer if it was reddish brown in colour. The other most common deer is the fallow deer, which is more yellowish brown with white spots. They both prefer forest habitats. The young are called fawns and are born in May and June. They can stand within 2 hours of being born.

**Red Deer**

# A Siege on Berkeley Castle

The castle was built in 1153 by Lord Maurice Berkeley, and it has been the home of the Berkeley family ever since. The castle has changed over the centuries from a Norman fortress, complete with dungeon, into a stately home with many superb paintings, tapestries, furniture and ornaments. You can see the cell where King Edward was murdered in 1327 or wander through the beautiful gardens and visit the butterfly farm. Something for all tastes! The castle is open from April to October and there is an admission charge. This walk cautiously circles the castle, passing right under its nose but then heading off across the fields to come upon it from the other side. Arm yourself ... and prepare for attack!

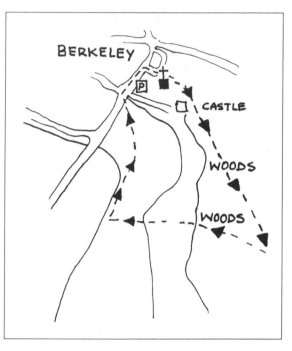

| | |
|---|---|
| **Starting point:** | High Street, Berkeley. Berkeley village is off the A38, south of Gloucester. As you enter the village turn left down High Street and park anywhere on the left-hand side. |
| **Distance:** | 2½ miles |
| **Terrain:** | Field paths, flat with lots of stiles |
| **Map:** | O.S. Landranger 162 |
| **Refreshments:** | Various shops and restaurants in Berkeley |

1. **Walk back up High Street and turn right into Church Lane. Pass the cottage on the left with the plaque by the gate.**

Q: Who lived in the cottage and why was he important?

A: Jenner, 1749-1823, discovered that vaccination prevented disease. In 1796 the first smallpox vaccination was given.

2. **Turn right into the churchyard. Follow the path round to the left and down a narrow passage.**

☺ Go quietly – so the castle guards don't hear you!

3. **Go through a doorway in the wall and down the path alongside the fence. Cross the stream and turn right at the corner of the copse and cross to the stile.**

☺ You are moving away from the castle, although so far you won't have been able to see it. But they may have seen you!

4. **Climb over the stile and go across the field to a green gate. Go over two gates and into a field. This field was very overgrown when we walked through, but the path goes straight across the middle to a stile in the hedge, next to a dead tree.**

☺ This field had maize growing in it during our walk (July '96). It was so tall it was high above our heads. We were like Pocahontas running through the maize field. It would provide good cover from those castle guards!

5. **Walk straight across the next field to a stile. Turn right and walk along the fence to a gate.**

☺ If you look straight ahead from the stile you can see the Tyndale Monument far away, high on the hill.

6. **Over a gate, turn right and walk alongside the copse.**

☺ Look out for a suitable battering ram for the castle gate! As you round the corner of the copse, the castle finally comes into view.

**Berkeley Castle**

7. **Go through a gateway, cross the bridge and turn left to walk along the edge of the field. Cross another bridge and continue to a gateway.**

☺ Crossbows at the ready! Look out for longbows!

8. **Turn right through a gate. Walk straight along, following the stream. Go over a stile and into the next field, still following the course of the stream.**

☺ Look for bulrushes and other water-loving plants and animals.

9. **Walk through a gateway and turn left.**

☺ This is a popular swimming spot for local children.

10. **Walk straight across the field to a stile by a gate in the far right-hand corner. This emerges on to a lane. Turn right and walk straight up back to the car.**

☺ You have now completely encircled the castle and so should have a good idea of how best to attack. Watch out for boiling oil!

## Other Attractions

The Jenner museum is in the town itself, but if you still have lots of energy try Cattle Country, outside Berkeley on the B4066. As well as some very interesting breeds of cattle, there is a brilliant adventure playground which is adult sized, too.

# A Walk To Rapunzel's Tower – Tyndale Monument, North Nibley

This is the tower, monument to the martyr William Tyndale, which dominates so many views of Gloucestershire. It stands high on the hill, amidst a forest, above the village of North Nibley. From three sides there seems to be only a tiny window at the top, hence the naming of it as Rapunzel's tower by six year old Maisie. It is quite a climb up there but the views across the county are worth the effort. If you start late morning, then the monument provides an early shady spot for lunch. You'll have butterflies as

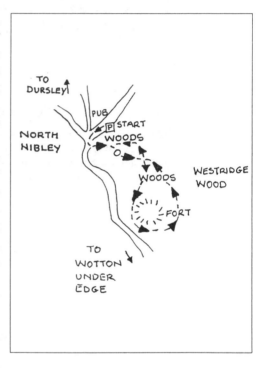

your mealtime companions in the summer though, due to the abundance of nettles. You can also go inside the monument, a sign at the beginning of the path, in the village, tells you where the key is available from. There is an admission charge. Also on the walk is the site of an old hill fort, dating back to the Iron Age, approximately 6th century BC. The only evidence of it is a shaped mound, now covered in trees, but you can look out across the valley as early man would have done thousands of years ago, possibly on the lookout for invaders coming up the River Severn. They certainly picked a good vantage point.

| | |
|---|---|
| **Starting point:** | North Nibley village, which is off the B4060, off the A38 going south from Gloucester. There are various on-road parking spaces in the village, by the pub, The Black Horse Inn, and outside the cemetery. |
| **Distance:** | 2 miles |
| **Terrain:** | Woodland tracks, steps, some steep ups and downs. |
| **Map:** | O.S. Landranger 162 |
| **Refreshments:** | Pub in the village with garden |
| **Pushchairs:** | If you are able to carry it up the first bit, then the rest of the route is easily suitable for pushchairs. |

1. **The path up to the monument is off the main road through the village, the B4060, between the Black Horse Inn and the cemetery. It is opposite a red telephone box and is marked by footpath signs and a large white sign with details of the key to the monument.**

2. **Very soon after starting along the path are some steps on the right, with a handrail.**

☺ Can you count how many steps there are all the way to the top? Halfway up you may have to go over, under or around a fallen tree!

3. **Keep on going up and up and up. Go over a stile at the top. The monument is straight in front, up one more short, slippery climb.**

☺ Walk around the tower checking out the amazing views. Look for butterflies, and birds of prey hovering out over the hillside.

Q: Can you read the plaque on the side of the tower above the door. It is quite difficult as it is so worn and weathered.

A: It reads: Erected in 1866 in grateful remembrance of William Tyndale, translator of the English Bible, who first caused the New Testament to be printed in the Mother Tongue of his countrymen. Born near this spot, he suffered martyrdom at ? Flanders on Oct 6th 1536. (If you can fill in the missing word, well done!)

North Nibley was the birthplace of William Tyndale whose translation of the scriptures is the basis of the Bible we use today. He was strangled and burned. The monument is 111feet high and stands 700 feet (215 metres) up the escarpment so it is visible for many miles around.

☺ The types of butterflies you are most likely to see are painted ladies, small tortoiseshells, red admirals and gatekeepers. They are attracted to flowers and found in most places. Painted ladies are the world's most common butterfly and among the most widely distributed insect on earth. The red admiral can fly at speeds of 25km per hour.

Among birds of prey you are most likely to see sparrow hawks, buzzards and kestrels (they're the ones you often see hovering by the sides of motorways). Birds of prey hunt other animals, catching them alive. True birds of prey have sharp talons and

**Kestrel**

hooked beaks. They are well known for their superb eyesight. See them soar in the air, hover, then drop on to their prey.

4. **Follow the path away from the monument, along the edge of the hill.**

☺ Close by is a stone with a topography set in the top. This shows you what you can see across the valley and how far away it is.

5. **Continue along the path and enter woods. Pass through a gateway, over a large stone slab.**

☺ Look out for butterflies.

6. **There are lots of paths here, going in all directions. Keep to the main path to the right and continue straight. A bridleway is marked by a blue arrow on a tree to the left. Continue straight on out on to an open track along the edge of the hill.**

7. **The path briefly re-enters the woods then goes back out into the open. On a sunny day it can get very hot and exposed. Wear a hat!**

☺ The path is gently curving around the site of an old hill fort. It is not possible to see it, but you can look out on the same view as your early ancestors.

8. **The path continues to curve round to the left. Near the end of it is a path that goes sharply down to the right. Continue straight past. Take the next left path.**

9. **At a fork, go right.**

☺ You can now see a mound of earth on your left amongst the trees. This is the site of the fort. If you carefully leave the path and walk along, you can see the shape of the fort. It consists of a ditch and bank enclosure.

10. **At a path crossroads continue straight. The path then rejoins**

the main path from point 6. Retrace your steps over the stone slab, through the woods and out into the open.

11. Now, either retrace your steps back to the monument and back down the steps in points 4, 3 and 2, or, and it makes little difference in distance, take the path straight across the grass and enter the woods through an open gateway.

12. The path goes quite steeply downhill and through another gateway. Continue straight ahead.

☺ You may see people climbing the steps up to the monument, to your left.

13. Pass the beginning of the steps on your left and emerge back on to the road where you began.

# *Follow the Line – Laverton*

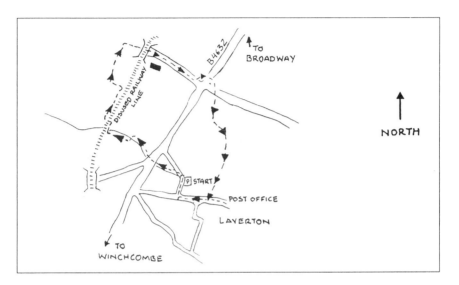

There is an echo of my own childhood in this walk as it incorporates a short distance along a disused railway line. My father was very keen on steam and liked to walk down the old tracks. Due to the cheapness of private car use, there was a large reduction of the rail network in the early 1960s, which left behind trackbeds and grassy embankments to flourish as unofficial nature reserves. The species that had survived while the line was in use remain, while other species can reclaim old haunts. There should be lots to look out for, so stoke up, blow your whistle and chug off to see what you can see.

| | |
|---|---|
| **Starting point:** | Laverton village, on the very edge of Gloucestershire. Laverton is on the B4632 north of Winchcombe, just before Broadway. Park on the road as you enter the village from the B4632, just past the Children at Play signs and the beginning of the footpath. |
| **Distance:** | 2 miles |
| **Terrain:** | Very flat, field paths, a short stretch on a quiet lane and a main road to cross. |
| **Map:** | O.S. Landranger 150 |

1.  Walk back along the lane to a stile on the left. Go over the stile and into the field. Turn left, following a fence and a line of trees to a kissing gate in a new fence.

☺ Look out for sheep in the fields.

2.  Continue straight, following the fence, and pass a water treatment works. Go over the stile on the left. Be careful on emerging as this is the main road.

3.  Cross the main road and follow the footpath over a narrow footpath opposite.

☺ Who's under the bridge? Remember *The Three Billy Goats Gruff*?

4.  Continue straight, walking away from the road alongside the brook. Follow the yellow arrows to cross over the brook and continue along next to it.

☺ Look out for rose hips in winter, or the beautiful wild rose in summer, though they flower only briefly. Rose hips are rich in vitamin C and were collected, by children, during the Second World War to produce rose hip syrup – a necessary vitamin supplement for war time.

5.  Continue towards the footbridge up ahead.

☺ Pass a horse chestnut tree. The horse part of the name comes from the Turks who used parts of the tree as medicine for their horses.

6.  Cross the footbridge and go over the stone stile on the left.

☺ See lichen growing on the stile. Lichen is a sign that the air is clean in the area as lichen cannot survive in polluted areas.

7.  Tackle a short, steep climb to emerge on the disused railway line. Turn right and follow the line.

☺ In summer the track should be bordered by a mass of tall pink flowers. This is rosebay willowherb.

8. **Walk along the track, passing a No. 9 sign.**

☺ Disused railway lines support a variety of birds, animals and plants. Plants will vary according to the soil and climate of the area. The embankment grass will have been left alone since the closure so may be overgrown but now provides shelter for wood mice, shrews and voles.

Look for kestrels hovering over the grassy embankments looking for those mice and voles. In the summer there should be a variety of butterflies.

**Rosebay Willowherb**

9. **At the No. 8 marker, turn left and go down through a gateway. Turn right and through another gate. Continue straight.**

☺ See the teasels growing by the No. 8 sign. These are a favourite food for goldfinches.

10. **Continue straight to another gate and across the field towards a low barn.**

☺ Look for rabbits. The soft soil of the embankments provide excellent burrows. If they live here, so do foxes.

We saw a green woodpecker fly across the field in front of us, so keep your eyes peeled for a flash of yellow and green.

**11. Go through a metal barred gate and turn right on to the lane. Go under the railway bridge.**

☺ You are now passing under the railway line you were just walking on. Look back as you come out from under the bridge to see the flood depth gauge on the side of the road.

**12. Continue up the lane, passing Little Buckland Farm on the right.**

☺ See the old farm buildings and lichen-covered, slate-tiled roofs.

Q: Can you remember what it means if lichen is growing somewhere?

A: See point 6, page 69.

☺ On the left is a horse exerciser and lots of horses in the surrounding fields.

**13. At the top of the lane cross over the verge before the Give Way sign, and then walk over the main road and down the lane signposted to Buckland.**

**14. Ahead on the right is the footpath sign. Go over a stile, straight across the field. Walk past a line of coppiced trees and turn left to a stile along the left-hand side of the field.**

☺ Look out for large black birds. Can you recognise if they are rooks, ravens or crows? (See Nympsfield walk)

**15. Walk across the next field, bearing to the right to join a gravel path. Follow this through a gateway.**

☺ Look for tiny flashes of colour flitting through the hawthorn bushes and see if you can see tits, chaffinches and bullfinches.

16. Continue straight along the gravel path towards the houses of Laverton village.

17. Pass two footpath signs and continue straight past an old drystone wall.

☺ Look for geese to the right and an old red telephone box on the left.

18. Emerge on to the main street of Laverton village.

☺ In the garden of the house opposite is a fig tree. See its large hand-shaped leaves.

19. If you turn left you can have a look at the old post office with its low, beamed ceiling and old scales, still in use today.

☺ Opposite is a house with a bell tower. When you walk past the house and see the front you will see the name, The Old School House.

Q: What do you think the bell was used for?

20. From the post office and school house, retrace your steps back to the end of the footpath and continue straight through the village. Turn right down the lane to return to the starting point of the walk.

## Other Attractions

If your enthusiasm for railways is still well stoked then you are in luck because there are two more attractions very close by. The Gloucestershire and Warwickshire Railway is based at Toddington, 3 miles north of Winchcombe, straight down the B4632 out of Laverton, following the 'train' signs. You will find a restored station, signal box and goods shed. Steam trains run on weekends and Bank Holidays from March to October on a 10 mile round trip. Special events include visits from Father Christmas in December and

Thomas the Tank Engine and Friends throughout the year. So make their day by meeting Thomas *in person*. Different charges for admission, rides and events.

In Winchcombe itself, there is the Winchcombe Railway Museum and Garden. Here you can see what it was like in the days of steam through a huge collection of exhibits. The museum is open from Easter to October, Saturday, Sunday and Bank Holidays 1.30 to 5.30pm, also Wednesday, Thursday and Friday 10am to 2pm, and daily throughout August 1.30 to 5.30pm. There is an admission charge.

# From Weir to Weir – across the Severn Ham

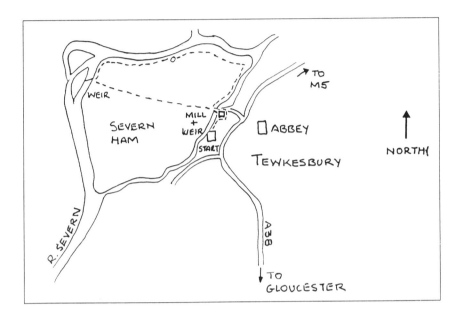

Tewkesbury is a lovely old town on the northern border of Gloucestershire. The town has grown up around the abbey, first founded in the 8th century. On the main street are some fine old medieval buildings. It is a town well worth viewing under any circumstances, but for children, who may not be so keen on the abbey, timbered buildings and quaint alleyways, not to mention a variety of highly browsable shops, this walk takes them out into the open to enjoy a different view of the town. For here is where the Severn meets the Avon so the walk follows the banks of two rivers. The two rivers and the sluice that powered the mill, called the Mill Avon, form an island known as the Severn Ham. This is agricultural land so there may be sheep or cows grazing here. At the mill is an adjustable weir, and across the Severn is another, longer one, so you have double the crashing, foaming and thundering water. Look for water birds and keep your eyes peeled for rabbits, you should not be disappointed.

**Starting point:** Pay and Display car park. If you approach the town along the A38 from Gloucester, then the car park is on the left as you enter the town, before the abbey. Tewkesbury can also be reached from the M5 at Junction 9. Drive through the centre of town, past the abbey to the car park. It costs 75p for up to 4 hours Mon-Sat and is free on Sundays. (1997 prices)

**Distance:** 1½ miles

**Terrain:** Very flat, open pathways

**Map:** O.S. Landranger 150

**Toilets:** At the car park

**Refreshments:** Various in town. The old mill is now a restaurant. There is also an excellent tea room, The Abbey Refectory, next to the abbey, which is open all year and can provide a highchair.

**Pushchairs:** Suitable for pushchairs

**Tewkesbury Weir**

1.  **In the corner of the car park, to the left of the toilet block, is a black signpost pointing to the river. Follow this down to the riverside gardens.**

☺ Can you hear the weir already?

2.  **Through the gardens and you will see the weir next to the mill.**

☺ It looks like a mini waterfall. Can you see the waterwheel?

3.  **Walk around the mill and turn left at its corner to cross over the weir.**

☺ A mill was first built here in 1190 and rebuilt in 1793. There is an information board on the bridge. It shows how the level of the weir can be lowered to prevent flooding. As you cross the bridge, see if you can see the 'arm' that does this.

4.  **Go through a gate, passing another information board which tells you about the piece of land known as the Severn Ham.**

☺ The Ham is agricultural land and used for grazing in the autumn, so there may be sheep or cows to walk around.

5.  **Walk straight across the grass to the trees opposite.**

☺ See the boat sign ahead of you in the distance. When you are about halfway across you will be able to hear the thundering of the water. It is also worth turning back to look at the town of Tewkesbury behind you with the distinctive short, square tower of the abbey.

6.  **At the river's edge is a bench, and down below is the weir on the river Severn.**

☺ A weir is a man-made construction to control the flow of the river.

7. **Turn right and walk along the path alongside the river, away from the weir.**

☺ It is amazing how quickly the sound of the water fades away. See the boat sign that directs boats around the weir to the lock. A lock is like an enclosure for boats to go in and join another section of river of a different level. Can you see the traffic lights for boats?

8. **Continue through some trees and out next to a big boat sign. Continue straight along the riverbank.**

☺ Look out for a variety of water-loving birds – swans, moorhens and ducks. Mute swans in Britain have been the property of the King or Queen since the 12th century and are protected. The county border runs down the river at this point so the opposite bank is in Worcestershire. Look for the sign 'Welcome to the River Avon.'

9. **Ahead of you is a fenced off earth mound.**

☺ The mound is actually an underground reservoir but, more importantly, it is Rabbit City. The bank is riddled with burrows and you should see lots of rabbits running for the safety of the metal fence. A rabbit warren is a complicated network of tunnels. The rabbits will all dig together and can cover a huge area, with many exits and entrances. There may well be rabbits beneath your feet!

10. **Continue on towards the factory buildings and round them to the right, passing some animal pens. Continue straight towards a fenced off tree plantation and towards a green bridge.**

☺ Look for gulls perched on the bridge and ducks and swans on the water below. There is an information board by the bridge.

11. **Do not cross the bridge, but turn right and walk along the path.**

☺ See the moorings for private boats.

12. **Continue straight back to the white bridge over the first weir. From the mill corner retrace steps 3, 2 and 1 back to the car park or walk straight up the road towards the abbey for the town, the Abbey Refectory and various other refreshment options.**

## Other Attractions

The John Moore Countryside Museum can be found on Church Street and has a large collection of natural history displays. It raises awareness of the need for conservation. Live animal events are held regularly where various creatures can be seen and even handled. There is also a collection of giant wildlife sculptures by Alan Jack, made from recycled metals. Open April to Oct, Tues to Sat and Bank Holidays. Admission charge.

# *Gloucester Docks – A City Walk*

This is not a city walk in that it takes you around the streets of Gloucester, but rather that it takes you out of Gloucester and circles around it so you are never far from it. An urban landscape is spread before you, car parks, railway tracks, playing fields, telephone poles, pylons and two electricity transformers. But amongst it all are butterflies and birds, plants and insects, grassy meadows and marshy wastelands. The walk starts and finishes at Gloucester Docks, a place of great historical interest with much to see and do. The port is home to many kinds of boats and the buildings are home to various museums and shops as well as the city council offices. There are numerous information boards and plaques on the buildings so you should never be at a loss for what, why, who and where.

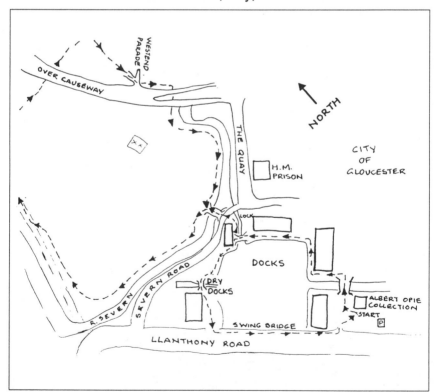

**Starting point:** The Robert Opie Museum of Advertising and Packaging at Gloucester Docks. Gloucester is on the A38 north of Bristol and the Docks are in the city centre. Follow the brown signs with the anchor on them. There is a Pay and Display Car Park at the Docks which costs £1.80 for 2 to 4 hours. Sunday, £1 all day. (1997 prices)

**Distance:** 2½ miles

**Terrain:** Very flat grassy paths, will be muddy after rain

**Map:** O.S. Landranger 162

**Toilets:** Next to the National Waterways Museum

**Refreshments:** Various options at the Docks or in the city centre, only a minute's walk away.

**Gloucester Docks**

1.  **Turn right at the Robert Opie Museum and walk across the swing bridge. Turn left, passing the Merchants Quay Shopping centre, and right past the Pizza Piazza. Walk along the dockside and turn left at the end.**

☺ Look out for swans. There is usually a small group of them. The young can be recognised by their grey/brown plumage, though they are the same size as the adults.

North Warehouse is on your right. Can you see the bell on the corner?

Q: What is the bell called?

2.  **Walk past the dock crane to the footbridge over the lock.**

Q: Look at the chart on the crane. How much can be lifted on a single hook?

3.  **Turn right at the Antiques Centre. The lock is on your right.**

☺ A lock is an enclosure for raising and lowering boats so they can join another waterway of a different level.

4.  **Go out through the white gates and cross the road to the footbridge opposite. Take extreme care as this is an awkward road to cross.**

☺ The bridge crosses the River Severn. Look down at its swirling currents.

5.  **Turn left at the end of the bridge and then left again down some steps between wooden railings. Follow the path to the right along the river bank.**

☺ In summer look for butterflies in the long grass.

6.  **Pass an arrowed post and continue straight. Pass a wooden bench, walking towards the bridge, turn right just before it.**

☺ You have started to leave the noise of the city behind you, but it is never far away. If you look over to the right, you can always see the Cathedral.

7. **Continue straight on at the fork, gradually getting higher.**

☺ Look out for rabbits.

8. **Walk alongside the disused railway tracks. Cross a bridge, go under a tangle of telephone wires, and continue until the path joins the railway line. Walk down the tracks.**

☺ Disused railway lines support a variety of birds, animals and plants. The most common railway plant is rosebay willowherb which is tall and pink. There are also blackberry bushes growing here. In the summer the rails will get quite hot and so should attract a variety of insects. If you are lucky you may see a lizard enjoying the sun. Moss growing between the stones makes a soft carpet underfoot. Be careful if you are walking on the sleepers as they will be slippery when wet.

9. **Continue along the tracks. The playing fields are to your right.**

☺ Across the fields is an electricity transformer. It's not pretty but without it there would be no television!

10. **Continue across a crossing between two gates. Walk beside the tracks as they are quite overgrown.**

☺ Look to the left to see grazing land and a bend in the River Severn. Look for birds in the hedgerows, blue tits and goldfinches especially.

11. **Go over a bridge and continue along the tracks.**

☺ Look for seagulls flocking on to the marshy ground over to the left. The correct name for seagull is 'herring gull'. From master fishers they have become excellent scavengers, taking advantage of man's rubbish. A captive herring gull lived for 44 years.

12. **The tracks widen out, choose to walk alongside them or carry on along them.**

☺ Look for rosehips in the winter. These were collected, as a valuable source of vitamin C, by children in the Second World War.

Look also for blackbirds and magpies. Magpies are very distinctive, easy-to-spot birds. They are not well liked by bird lovers as they steal other birds' eggs. They will also steal shiny objects and hide them by burying them.

13. **Another electricity transformer is on the left. Cross the tracks towards a metal gate on the right.**

☺ The rails are good for budding gymnasts, but take care! In contrast to the hard rails, the moss next to them is very soft. Look to the right to see an old, red brick bridge with a small river flowing beneath it.

14. **Cross through the fence just before the gate and walk up on to a concrete path. Go over the stile in front of you to walk under the main road.**

☺ See the cars overhead. Can you make echoes under the bridge?

15. **Walk towards the ten arches of the old, brick bridge, but when the path joins a wider, gravel path join that and turn right heading back towards the road.**

16. **Pass round a wooden gate by climbing up the bank to the left of it. Follow the path to another gate. Go through this and cross the road, Westend Parade.**

☺ Look for blackberries along this path in September.

17. **Walk along the pavement next to the main road and follow the footbridge sign to Gloucester down past some houses parallel with the road. Turn to the right at the fence with the yellow arrows on it to cross under the first carriageway.**

☺ Look for the Shire horse which belongs to the National

Waterways Museum, but is often to be found grazing in the fields here. A Shire horse can weigh over a tonne and pull up to five times its own weight.

18. **Go past the footbridge to the city centre to go under the second carriageway of the road. Then go through a kissing gate marked by a yellow arrow.**

☺ If the horse is not in the field you may see his hoofprints. They are enormous!

19. **Go straight across the field towards that transformer again.**

☺ Can you see the dock buildings up ahead?

20. **The riverbank is on your left, follow it to a kissing gate.**

☺ Look for water birds.

21. **Continue through another gate into another field.**

☺ There should be sheep here, and in the spring, lambs.

22. **Walk along the edge of the field next to the river.**

☺ The new brick building with the shiny windows up ahead is Gloucester Prison.

23. **Walk past a sign for boats.**

☺ Look for the masts at the docks. The hill behind is Robinswood Hill and over to the left is the Cathedral. Above the noise of traffic see if you can hear birds singing.

24. **Either go over a stile and back over the bridge in points 4 and 5 then retrace your steps to the car park or**

25. **From the Antiques Centre go straight on to walk along the other side of the docks to see the dry docks.**

☺ There is often a boat or two in the dry dock undergoing

restoration or repair,and it is fascinating to see such a different view.

**26. Continue on up to a road, past the Furniture Recycling Warehouse and turn left on to the road to cross the swing bridge.**

☺ If you are lucky you might see the swing bridge in action. It rises straight up in the air to allow boats to pass in and out of the docks. If a boat does go through, don't forget to wave!

**27. Turn left down some steps just after the bridge to return to the car park and the docks.**

## Other Attractions

At the Docks – The Robert Opie Museum of Advertising and Packaging. Possibly a little too nostalgic for the young, though older children may be interested in the changes. Open daily. Admission charge.

The Soldiers of Gloucestershire Regimental Museum tells the story of the county's regiments and includes a life-size reconstruction of a First World War trench. Open June to Sept. Admission charge.

The National Waterways Museum is in the Victoria Warehouse and has three floors of exhibits. It is absolutely fascinating with lots to see and do. Open daily. Admission charge.

In Gloucester – behind the prison, which you will see on the walk, is Gloucester Prison Museum which is housed in the Old Gate Lodge of the original prison building. Its only small but very interesting. Open from Easter Tuesday to the end of Sept. Small admission charge.

The Gloucester Folk Museum is just a short walk away from the Docks and has many exhibits of local history, folklore and crafts. The Victorian schoolroom is fascinating. Open daily. Admission free.

If adults want to see the Cathedral, then make sure you go there via the Beatrix Potter Shop and Museum. In here is absolutely everything you might possibly want with Peter Rabbit on it! The shop itself was the model for the Tailor of Gloucester shop.

# 𝒯𝒉𝒆 𝓛𝒐𝒏𝒈 𝓑𝒂𝒓𝒓𝒐𝒘 – 𝓑𝒆𝒍𝒂𝒔 𝓚𝒏𝒂𝒑𝒑

Belas Knapp is a long barrow, or burial mound, with four chambers and one false entrance. When it was first discovered, the chambers contained 38 human skeletons, some animal remains and some tools and pottery dated at around 2000BC. It is a very big mound and it is possible to enter the chambers, which are like mini-caves and quite fascinating for children. There is an excellent information board and map of the mound at the site. This walk is a circular walk, though you can walk straight up to the

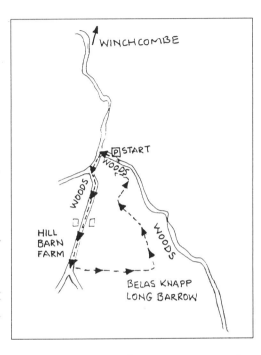

mound and back again along the same route. Our route enters the mound from the opposite side to the direct route so that as you walk towards it, it is in sight all the way. Both routes involve a long hill climb, there is no avoiding that!

---

**Starting point:** Take the B4632 out of Prestbury towards Winchcombe and follow the signs to Belas Knapp. Park on the road by the brown sign pointing towards the woods. There is an obvious parking area on the side of the road.

**Distance:** 2 miles

**Terrain:** Lanes, tracks, field paths and woods. Hilly.

**Map:** O.S. Landranger 163

---

1.  **Walk back down the lane. Turn left up the lane signposted Corndean Lane and West Downs.**

😊 Look across the valley, to the right. Can you see Sudeley Castle?

2.  **At the fork go left towards Hill Barn Farm.**

😊 It is quite a climb. Look for blackberries in September.

3.  **Keep on going up the lane. Eventually some farm buildings, Hill Barn Farm, will come into view and fields will open up to the right.**

😊 Look for sheep and horses and a variety of field birds, especially magpies. We know magpies for their thievery of bright objects and for the childhood rhyme, *One for sorrow, two for joy*, but they also have an unpleasant reputation amongst bird lovers for stealing from other birds' nests.

4.  **Continue through Hill Barn Farm.**

😊 Look for chickens and a rooster.

5.  **The road becomes a track and continues on straight from the farm, between two fields. Turn left at the footpath sign pointing to Belas Knapp.**

😊 From the footpath sign the long barrow is in sight all the way.

6.  **Walk straight towards the barrow along the edge of the field. Go over a stone stile.**

😊 On the left is a map of the barrow set into the wall, and an information board. Have a good look around the mound.

7.  **To leave the barrow, exit over the stone stile opposite the one you entered over. Turn left, through a kissing gate, and turn left again out towards the edge of the field. Turn right and walk along the line of hawthorn bushes.**

**The Long Barrow**

☺ Look for tits and finches in the hawthorn as this is a popular habitat for them.

8.  Continue along the boundary of the field. Look for Sudeley Castle again when the view opens out to the right. Look for the buildings of Hill Barn Farm over to the left.

9.  Follow the line of the drystone wall round to a kissing gate. Continue down the field, following the line of the wall.

☺ The town of Winchcombe is in front of you. Can you see the church?

10. Continue on down the hill, following the wall to the fence at the bottom and then left along the edge of the woods. About three-quarters of the way along is a kissing gate. Go through this and follow the path through the woods to the stile at the bottom. Once over the stile, you are back at the starting point.

# 'Water, water everywhere . . .'
# Cotswold Water Park

The Park is the largest
concentration of
man-made fresh water
lakes in Britain. The
gravel beds were
formed at the time of
the Great Ice Age as
the ice ground the rock
to gravel. During the
1920s and 30s the pits
were dug for gravel but
water kept seeping in.
Eventually, lakes were
formed which now
provide rich habitats
for a variety of
water-loving plants
and animals. It is also
a centre for

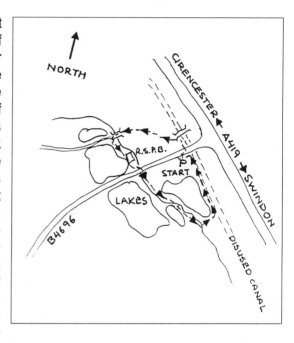

water-based sports and recreation. You should see many different
types of water birds, from ducks and coots to cormorants and swans.
But other lake life include jet skiers, windsurfers and all kinds of boats.

**Starting point:** Take the A419 out of Cirencester towards Swindon and
follow signs to the Cotswold Water Park. The starting
point is the car park off the B4696.

**Distance:** 2 miles

**Map:** O.S. Landranger 163

**Terrain:** Grassy tracks, will be muddy after rain. Very flat.

**Toilets:** At the starting point, in the car park.

1.  **Walk back out of the car park. Turn right and cross the road to the public footpath sign to South Cerney, above a Thames and Severn Canal sign. Go down some steps, across a narrow bridge and walk alongside the canal.**

☺ The Thames and Severn Canal was completed in 1789. It is 37 miles long and had 57 locks.

The canal linked the River Thames to the River Severn. It was very busy until 1845 when a railway line was built linking Gloucester to Swindon. The last boat passed through in 1911, and the canal was finally abandoned in 1927.

2.  **At the bridge, go over the stile by the gate and turn left, following the sign to South Cerney.**

☺ When we walked through, the bridge and lock were being restored in line with the plan to completely restore the entire canal. In ten years time there should be boats on the canal again.

3.  **Follow the wide, grassy track away from the bridge.**

☺ To the left is a lake, though it is difficult to see over the blackberry bushes. You should see birds flying overhead though. There are lots of rabbit holes and blackbirds darting in and out of the brambles. The male blackbird is very familiar with its jet black feathers and bright yellow beak, but its duller mate with her brown feathers and speckled chest has often been mistaken for a song thrush.

4.  **Go over a stile and along a narrower path alongside a ditch.**

☺ Listen out for bird calls. You may see blue tits, great tits, finches, magpies and crows. We heard the honking of geese and even saw a jay.

5.  **At the metal gate go over the stile and follow the track round to the white bridge.**

☺ Just before the white bridge are some steps down to a narrow bridge. Which one will you choose to cross the River Churn?

6.  **Turn left, pass a post with yellow arrows and continue straight on to a metal gate and a large lake opening out in front.**

☺ Go down the bank and investigate the River Churn and the small weir built to control its flow.

What birds can you see on the lake? The European coot is named for its long high-pitched cry. The coot is easily recognisable with its black feathers and white forehead and bill. It is extremely aggressive and will defend its breeding territory, using water spray to scare off birds of prey, while diving for cover.

7.  **Continue straight ahead.**

☺ On the left look for the large tree bending out across the river and with another branch forming an arch. With parental guidance it's safe to explore. See the bulrushes at the edge of the lake.

8.  **Before turning the corner the path spreads out down to the water's edge.**

☺ Take care looking out across the water. See the island and the birds. Look for cormorants in the trees on the island. Cormorants have roughened beaks so as to hold on better to a slippery fish. They will swim underwater with only their head and neck above the surface. In parts of China and Japan they are used by people to catch fish – a ring on their necks preventing them from swallowing the fish themselves, and on a lead so they'll come back.

9.  **Walk past the RSPB building and Outdoor Education Centre. Pass the boats and holiday cabins and walk out on to the road, the B4696. Take care through the car park and on emerging on to the road as it is quite busy. There are toilets here.**

Q: What is the blue winch for, on the right just after the toilets?

10. **Turn left and cross the road to the bus stop and a public footpath sign pointing to Cerney Wick. Go down some steps and over a stile.**

11. **Follow the path up to the left, then immediately right to walk alongside the river.**

☺ See what is happening on the large lake on the other side of the river. We saw jet-ski racing.

Cormorant

12. **The path follows the line of the river and continues straight. Pass an active gravel pit on the left and a fishing lake on the right.**

13. **The path joins the track access to the gravel pit. Turn, following a yellow footpath arrow, across the bridge and left past the fishing lake.**

☺ Quiet, so as not to disturb the fish!!

14. **At the end of this lake, follow the path to the left through two wooden posts. Following the yellow arrow pointing straight on, go over a stile.**

15. **Turn left and go over a metal gate, following the footpath sign to the canal towpath. Walk over the concrete bridge and out towards the lake. Turn right and walk around the end of the lake.**

☺ Look for swans.

Q: What is a baby swan called?

A: A cygnet.

☺ There are seven species of swan and five of them are pure white. Mute swans carry their young on their backs.

Look for molehills. Moles can lift over twenty times their own weight of soil. They are almost completely blind and deaf and use their noses to detect vibrations, especially of worms which make up 90 per cent of their diet.

16. **You can see the roof of the toilet block at the starting point through the trees across the lake. In the corner there is a post with yellow arrows and a bridge. Cross the bridge and turn left, following the sign to South Cerney, 2miles.**

Q: Maths question! If South Cerney was 1.5 miles away from the car park and now it is 2 miles away from this bridge, how far do you have to walk to get back to the car?

A: Half a mile.

17. **Follow the old canal towpath.**

☺ This is the absolute border of Gloucestershire with Wiltshire. The muddy ditch to your right is the old canal.

18. **Continue along the narrow path.**

☺ Look out for the fallen tree which you can walk under.

19. **Cross a concrete bridge with a metal handrail. The road is in sight up ahead. Before the road, at the fence turn left to return to the starting point.**

### Other Attractions

Three miles south east of Cirencester, off the A419, is The Butts Farm, a rare farm animals' park. There is a play area, pets corner, picnic spot and shop. Admission charge. Open Easter to September, Wednesday to Sunday and Bank Holidays.

For more watery fun try the Keynes Country Park, 4 miles south of Cirencester, which can be reached by driving further along the B4696. Here you can walk, barbecue and play. There is even a children's beach for those hot summer days. Or you can walk some more, around the lake and through the nature reserve. Admission free, open all year, every day. Parking charge in the summer.

And, of course, there is Cirencester itself with its many Roman attractions, the remains of an amphitheatre, and the Corinium museum on Park Street which contains one of the country's biggest collections of Roman artefacts. Admission charge.

# *Stones, Balls and Water – Avening*

This walk starts in Avening, an ancient village with an 11th-century church, inside which is a monument to a notorious highwayman and pirate, the Hon. Henry Brydges. The walk goes away from the village, up a lane and past The Tingle Stone, a prehistoric stone covered in holes. You'll have to look carefully to spot it as you cannot get very close. Fore! The footpath goes straight across a golf course

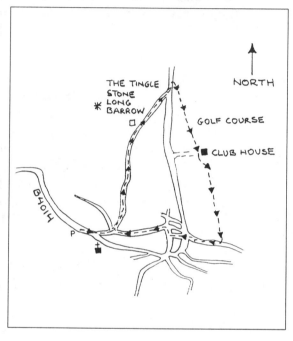

so watch for golf balls. There are lots of signs and arrowed posts to look for along the way. Unfortunately, the last section of the walk includes a short stretch along a narrow lane which has no footpath, so be warned if walking with young children.

---

**Starting point:**   Avening village, south of Nailsworth on the B4014. Park off the road on the right as you enter the village, just before the Murco petrol station, in front of a row of pretty stone cottages.

**Distance:**   2½ miles

**Map:**   O.S. Landranger 162

**Terrain:**   Lanes and fields, steep ups and downs

**Toilets:**   In the village hall, but access only when it is open

**Refreshments:**   Pubs in the village

---

1. **Cross the road from the parking place and turn right, walking towards the village.**

☺ See the church tower to the right.

2. **Turn left up Rectory Lane, opposite the Avening town sign and the entrance to the church. It's quite a climb!**

3. **Turn left at the fork and then go straight up the narrow, wooded lane.**

4. **At the houses, the lane becomes a path. Continue straight up.**

☺ Don't worry, the hill flattens out just past these houses. Look out at the view over the wall, across wooded hills.

5. **Continue along the path.**

☺ Look out for horse jumps. In the distance, on the hill, is a wind-power generator, a modern day windmill.

6. **Continue straight on past lots of horse jumps.**

☺ At the barn up ahead, look over the wall for the sheep dip. As you pass the hedge, look over to the left and amongst the trees is The Tingle Stone. Stones such as these are evidence of prehistoric man having lived in the area. This one marks the sight of a burial mound.

7. **Walk through a gateway and alongside a narrow copse. The road comes into sight up ahead.**

8. **Turn left and walk along the road, then cross over to the footpath on the right. Go over the wall with the help of the stone steps.**

9. **Turn right and walk across the field to a stone stile in a drystone wall. Climb over the stile and follow the line of the fence and wall.**

☺ Can you see any golfers or flags up ahead?

We saw a green woodpecker, easily recognised by its yellowy-green plumage, red head and undulating flight.

**Green Woodpecker**

10. **Go over a stone stile and on to the golf course. Follow the arrow on the post straight across towards the clubhouse.**

☺ Look out for golf balls! Look for 'Fairy Rings' in the grass. 'Fairy Rings' are dark circles in the grass. We like to think of them as where fairies have danced, but the scientific explanation of them is that a fungal colony has expanded across the grass, fertilising the soil as it goes so the grass is greener.

11. **At the line of trees see the sign warning walkers to beware of golf balls. To the right of this hedgerow is an arrowed post. Follow this arrow straight on.**

☺ Look out for the next arrows at the end of the hedge.

12. At the corner of the clubhouse is another arrowed post. Go straight across the car park and turn left at the next post. Follow the track round to the right.

13. Follow the track until it bends right and follow the arrow straight along a narrow, grassy path to a green barn.

14. Turn right after the barn and then follow the grassy track straight across the golf course.

☺ Look for the arrowed post at the gap in the wall. There is also a sign by it. Can you be the first to read it?

15. Follow the grassy track straight down to another post just over a hillock and go over the stile.

☺ See the town of Avening over to the right.

16. Continue down the steep hill, passing another arrowed post. A steep downhill walk leads to a gap in the fence next to a tall footpath sign.

☺ Look out for magpies. Magpies will dig holes to hide food or the bright objects they steal. Unfortunately, they also steal other birds' eggs so are not popular with bird lovers.

17. Careful down the steep steps on to the lane. Turn right and walk along the lane.

☺ Look down to the left for a narrow stream and weir. This stream runs through Avening and you will see it at several different points.

18. At the junction with the main road, cross straight over and follow the footpath to the left of the one-way lane. The path widens into a lane. Turn right at the bottom.

☺ Look out for the spring on the right, with steps leading down to it.

19. Turn left at the post box, down Rectory Lane.

☺ Look out over Avening to the left. There is also a playing field on the right past the houses, with some swings etc.

**20. Follow the lane to the main road at the end.**

☺ See the church tower straight ahead.

**21. At the main road, turn right for the starting point. However, it is worth a detour to cross the road and have a look at the church.**

☺ A bridge crosses the stream that you saw earlier. The primary school is on the left of the entrance to the church. Can you see the bell tower?

The churchyard has many old graves with worn headstones that it is no longer possible to read. The church itself dates back to the Normans. In the North Transept is the monument to the notorious Henry Brydges. It shows a man kneeling in prayer, not the sort of attitude you would expect from a known highwayman and pirate but, perhaps, an indication of his repentance in later years. Henry Brydges had his horses shod back-to-front so he could not be tracked. In 1611 he was granted a pardon for piracy by James 1st. He died in 1615.

# *'Walk in Beauty' – Bibury*

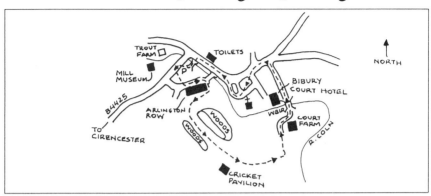

Called, 'The most beautiful village in England,' by William Morris, we also fell in love with Bibury instantly. Its natural attractions include the fast-flowing, sparkling River Coln and the variety of wildfowl on the central reserve. For the historically minded there is the row of 17th-century weavers' cottages known as Arlington Row which were converted from a 14th-century sheep barn. If you want to top your walk off with an educational visit, there is the Arlington Mill Museum and the Bibury Trout Farm where you can feed rainbow trout and then catch your own supper! Admission charge at both. This is a very short but extremely enjoyable walk.

| | |
|---|---|
| **Starting point:** | Bibury is north-east of Cirencester on the B4425. There is a parking area just past the Mill Museum, on the right before the bridge, with some useful tourist information. |
| **Distance:** | 1½ miles |
| **Map:** | O.S. Landranger 163 |
| **Terrain:** | Short uphill, woodland and field paths, tracks and pavement. |
| **Toilets:** | In the centre of the village |
| **Refreshments:** | There is a tea room, Jenny Wren's, in the village and also at the Mill Museum. |
| **Pushchairs:** | 95 per cent of this walk is very suitable. If you can manage the short section through the woods and over one stile, then go for it! |

1.  From the parking area, after you've read the tourist informa-
    tion, walk back towards the Mill Museum, but then turn left
    along the tarmac footpath following the sign to Arlington Row.

☺ The piece of land to your left is known as Rack Isle. It is
    now a wildfowl reserve so you should see lots of ducks.
    Please do not ignore the signs asking you not to feed the
    ducks. The Isle is called Rack because it was here that
    cloth was hung to dry on large racks.

2.  Cross the narrow plank bridge, turn left and Arlington Row is
    straight ahead. Walk along the front of the cottages.

☺ The building was originally for agricultural use, and was
    built in 1380 as a store or maybe a sheep house. In the
    17th century the row was converted to weavers' cottages.
    It is now owned by the National Trust.

3.  At the end of the row turn right, go through the wooden gate
    and into a small car park. Turn right again to follow the path
    along the back of Arlington Row and up some wide steps.

4.  Turn left at the top and follow the path through the trees. At
    the fork go straight to a stone stile. Once over the stile, continue
    straight alongside the wall.

☺ The trees you are walking under are beech trees.
    Underfoot may be beech nuts. The beech is a magnificent
    tree grown for its beauty and fine timber. The dense canopy
    allows little light through for small shrubs and undergrowth,
    but the tree itself supports insects, fungi and birds. Pigs
    used to be herded into beech woods in autumn to feed on
    the nuts.

5.  Continue straight ahead, passing a cricket pavilion and fenced
    off pitch on the right. Head for the wooden gate in the stone
    wall straight ahead.

☺ Can you see the river bending away in the distance?

6.  Go through the gate and follow the track down to the bottom.

Turn left following a bridleway sign and go through a wooden gate.

7. **Follow the lane down, passing Court Farm on the right. The lane bends to the right, and then to the left.**

☺ Can you hear the sounds of rushing water? As the lane bends to the left, look for the old grinding stones leaning against the wall. Up above them is a dovecote.

8. **Follow the lane straight up to the road.**

☺ See the weir on your left and plenty of ducks. The bridge is a good one for Pooh sticks. The grand building on the left is the Bibury Court Hotel which was once a fine, old country house, built in 1633.

9. **At the top the lane emerges on to the road so take care. Turn left on to the pavement.**

Q: What is the name of the house on the left?

Q: What does this suggest that the house may once have been?

A: A brewery.

10. **Continue along the pavement and at the turning left towards the hotel, cross over to pass the red telephone box and cross a small green, past a row of cottages. Continue straight down to the church at the bottom.**

☺ The site of the church dates from the 9th century, and the main building is 10th or 11th century but it has remained unchanged since the 15th century so none of it is less than 500 years old.

11. **Follow the road round to the right. It emerges alongside the main road, next to the river. Continue straight ahead and pass a small stone bridge with three arches.**

There are toilets across the road here.

**12. Continue straight alongside the river and then turn left over the wooden footbridge to return to the parking area.**

☺ Remember, do not feed the ducks as it causes an imbalance in the population of males to females, and, therefore, fighting between the males.

### Other Attractions

The Arlington Mill Museum has a gift shop and tea room which you can enter free of charge. From the tea room you can see mill machinery and there are various information cards around the room. In the museum itself, for which there is an admission charge, there are mill and agricultural exhibits.

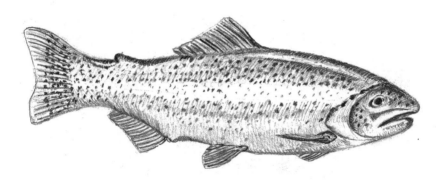

**Rainbow Trout**

The Bibury Trout Farm is a working trout farm which breeds rainbow trout. You can see them develop and also feed them. Gift shop and picnic area and a beautiful setting.

# 𝓔aster 𝓟arade! – 𝓜urrell's 𝓔nd, 𝓡edmarley

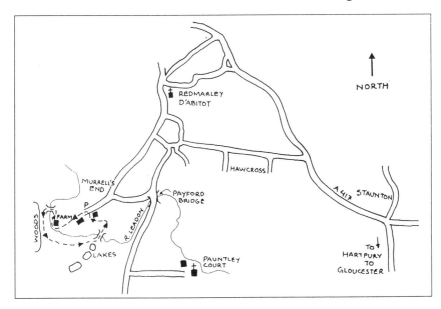

We recommend you do this walk around Easter time because then you should be treated to a glorious display of golden daffodils carpeting the woods. The walk also goes through a very old, small farmyard with red brick barns and lots of cows, chickens, geese and ducks. And if there are sheep, there may be lambs at Easter so this is definitely a walk that should have a Spring in its step!

| | |
|---|---|
| **Starting point:** | The middle of nowhere! Redmarley is a village off the A417, near Staunton, to the west of Tewkesbury, close to the M50 and the Gloucestershire border. The start of the walk, Murrell's End, is south of Redmarley down a dead end lane (see map). Go over the cattle grid and park just past the three footpath signs, off the track to the left, next to a very old sandstone wall. |
| **Distance:** | 1 mile only |
| **Map:** | O.S. Landranger 150 |
| **Terrain:** | Grass paths, will be muddy after rain, one hill climb |

1. **Walk straight ahead down the track.**

☺ Over the edge is a steep drop to the River Leadon in the gully.

2. **Continue straight down to the farm. Go through the gateway and follow the track round, passing the farmyard and farmhouse.**

☺ Look for the old barn with the round tower on the corner. Look also for chickens at the windows and cows in the barn. Domestic chickens are the most numerous birds on earth. They are descended from the jungle fowl in Asia which were originally domesticated for cock-fighting purposes. Farmyard chickens still behave similarly to their jungle ancestors, using their beaks and feet to rummage for insects in the soil.

3. **Go through the metal gate and over an old stone bridge. Turn left immediately after the bridge to walk along the edge of the river.**

☺ Look for rabbits in the woods. Rabbits were introduced by the Normans and farmed for their meat and fur. They are now considered an agricultural pest, especially since one doe can produce thirty young in eight months. Rabbits have over 17, 000 taste buds on their tongues.

4. **Passing the farm from across the river, continue straight ahead. Cross a wild clearing at the bottom of a hillside copse.**

☺ Look for wild daffodils in Spring.

**Wild Daffodil**

This area around Newent and the Gloucester/Hereford border is famous for its wild daffodil population. In the 1930s the railway ran weekend Daffodil Specials from London.

5.   **Go through a narrow gate tied with string.. Continue along the edge of the river towards the post and rail wooden bridge.**

☺ Opposite the bridge is a lovely pond. Look for bulrushes, coots and geese. Geese are often thought of as not quite a duck, not quite a swan, but somewhere in between. Actually, they are quite different, spending most of their time on land feeding on grasses.

6.   **Go across the bridge and walk straight up the hill until past the line of trees. Turn left.**

7.   **Bear left walking up the hill, following the line of trees. There should be a small cottage to the right.**

☺ At the hill plateau, look back over where you have walked. See the bridge and pond, and also another pond that has appeared.

8.   **Continue straight ahead, passing another house on the right, following a wire fence.**

9.   **Follow the line of this fence as it bears right, through the metal gate and back to the starting point.**

☺ See the old gate with the small grille 'window'.

### Other attractions

Nearby is Pauntley with its manor house and church, the home of generations of Whittingtons and probably the birthplace of that famous pantomime character, Dick. He was born around 1350 and did go to London to become Mayor several times. He did marry Alice Fitzwarren, the merchant's daughter, and died in 1423. Nobody is certain of whether there was a cat or not, one possible explanation is the Whittington coat of arms which has a black lion on it. If badly drawn, this could have been mistaken for a cat. The Whittington clan became established in Gloucester in 1311 when Richard's (Dick) great grandfather married the daughter who was heir to Pauntly. It is generally accepted that Richard was born here. Pauntley Court would not have been his home, but the nearby granary and dovecote might possibly have been there in his time. The chapel in the church was built by his family and the Whittington Arms are in the west window. A memorial to a more recent family member is in the porch. Become pantomime detectives for the day and discover the truth of the only pantomime character based on a historical person. Behind you!

# ℋistory in the Walking – Deerhurst

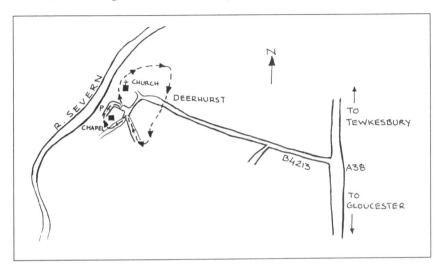

Deerhurst is a tiny village, no more than a hamlet, just south of Tewkesbury. The name means 'Forest of wild animals'. The place is remarkable for it is here, in this village in the county of Gloucestershire, that there is, possibly, the oldest dated church in all England. And only a few hundred yards away, an 11th-century Saxon chapel, known as Odda's chapel. In the 8th-century church there is plenty to look for. Scandinavian motifs show the Viking influence, there is a fine Saxon font and the famous Saxon carving, The Deerhurst Angel. The east window is thought to contain Roman stones.

Odda's chapel was founded in 1056 by Earl Odda, a friend of Edward the Confessor, in memory of his brother Elfric. For centuries it was forgotten and hidden within the walls of the adjoining farmhouse.

| | |
|---|---|
| **Starting point:** | Deerhurst village is three miles south of Tewkesbury off the A38. Follow signs to Deerhurst and Odda's chapel. Visitors' car park opposite the chapel – 50p for two hours. (1997) |
| **Distance:** | 1½ miles |
| **Map:** | O.S. Landranger 150 |
| **Terrain:** | flat, farmland paths |

1. **Go into the chapel first. On leaving, turn right and follow the
   lane back towards the church.**

☺ Pass the flood depth gauge on your left. This measures the
   height of water above sea level, in metres. How high before
   the water would be over your head? You will also pass
   through what looks like a stone gateway with two deep
   grooves cut into the stone. This is for sliding a heavy flood
   gate into.

2. **Go through the white gate into the churchyard and walk along
   the path to the church.**

☺ See the 14th -century priory on the right. Look for the
   golden cockerel weathervane on the top of the tower and
   the patches of irregular stonework in the walls. Look for
   gargoyles. There is a good example of the Saxon
   architectural method of 'long and short' corner stones on
   the tower.

3. **Have a look in the church.**

   The porch is 7th-century. In the church there are a variety of guides and
   post cards, including special sheets for children, for which modest
   payment is expected.

☺ Don't miss: the Font, probably the finest Saxon font in
   existence and the Cassey brasses with Terri, the dog,
   resting under Lady Alice's feet. This is possibly the only
   example of a named animal on a medieval brass.

4. **Turn right out of the church and follow the signs to the angel,
   which is round the back of the church. Then retrace your steps
   to the first To The Angel sign and walk across the grass to a
   wooden gate.**

5. **Go straight across to a stile marked by a yellow arrow, cross
   the track and go over a second stile.**

6. **Follow the direction of the arrow to the right and over another
   stile next to a metal gate.**

7. **Walk straight across, following the line of the hedge.**

☺ Look for tits and finches in the hedgerow. Hawthorn berries are a vital autumn food. Bullfinches are becoming common in hedgerows due to the loss of woodlands. Known and disliked for their raids on orchards, in the 16th century

**Bullfinch**

they had a bounty of one penny placed on their heads! Greenfinches sing at every opportunity, even in flight.

8. **Cross the** *Billy Goats Gruff* **style bridge.**

Q: Who's under the bridge?

A: A troll! Careful, don't look down.

9. **Go straight across the field to a stile next to a dead tree.**

☺ As this is farmland, look out for crows. Crows are easily recognised by their splayed wing tips in flight. They are very intelligent. Some have learned that when people are around other birds will leave their nests unprotected. The crow will take advantage to steal both eggs and young to eat.

10. **Do not go over the stile, but turn right just before it and go over another stile in the corner.**

Q: What does it say on the stone step of the stile?

11. **Follow the arrow and walk along the edge of the field up to the road.**

12. **Cross the road and go over the stile opposite.**

13. **Walk straight across the field to the stile at the end of the line of trees. Over this stile, turn right and walk along the edge of the field.**

☺ Look for animal holes under the hedge.

14. **Go over the next stile and continue straight ahead.**

☺ This is a pheasant farm and you should see birds in the coops, but take care not to disturb them. Look over to the right above the coops to the interesting chimneys of the house through the trees.

15. **Go over the stile at the end and turn right. At the metal gates turn right on to the track. Follow the track.**

☺ You will pass the house with the interesting chimneys.

16. **Continue straight on as the track becomes a lane, passing a farm and houses.**

17. **Turn left at the junction and walk up the lane, passing Deerhurst House.**

18. **Turn right at the footpath sign, climbing up on to the top of another floodgate holder.**

19. **Walk along the edge of the garden to the next stile.**

☺ See Odda's Chapel across to the right. You can see clearly how it is attached to the black and white timbered house.

20. **Go straight across the field, bearing right towards the chapel and a metal gate and trough. Go through the gate to return to the car.**

# *Other Places To Walk*

The following five places will provide you with an excellent day out but do not need a guided walk from us. The Country Parks have trails for you to follow and information boards to advance your knowledge of the area. Minchinhampton Common is such a wide open space it would be impossible to give directions for a walk around it.

## Minchinhampton Common

We went up there on a snowy day and though an icy wind whistled across the open common, we found shelter in the dips, lumps and bumps which also provided some excellent sledging terrain. On a warmer day the common is a great place to run about and has some interesting features to look for on its 240 hectares (600 acres). The Bulwarks are the remains of an Iron Age defence system. In the middle of the common, where the six roads meet, is Tom Long's Post. Here a gibbet once stood, as was common at crossroads so many people would see it. A notorious highwayman once swung from this one. Part of the common is a golf course so watch out for golfers. I hope you will find it a popular spot whatever the weather.

Getting there: Take the A46 out of Stroud heading south to Nailsworth, and follow signs to Amberley and then the Common.

Parking: You are allowed to park on the edge of the common.

## Robinswood Hill Country Park

The hill rises out of suburban Gloucester with 100 hectares (250 acres) of wood and grassland for you to explore. There are lots of paths to follow but make sure you reach the top so that you can look out over the whole of Gloucester. The hill was once a reservoir, providing the town with its water supply from natural springs. Now there are ponds and waterways. The visitor centre has lots of information, an excellent shop and has regular exhibitions. Open daily, admission free.

**Getting there:** 2 miles out of Gloucester city centre, off the A4173. Follow the signs.

**Parking:** Free car park on the hill.

## Coopers Hill

This hill is a wooded nature reserve on a hill overlooking the Severn Vale. You can follow a two-mile nature trail which includes points of archaeological interest. Of more interest, however, may be the fact that this is the place where the annual 'cheese rolling' takes place each May. This is an ancient ritual thought to assert the rights of the locals to graze their sheep here. People now race down the very steep slope in pursuit of Double Gloucester cheeses and try not to break their necks!

**Getting there:** The hill is off the A46 between Cheltenham and Stroud.

**Parking:** There is a car park.

## Dovers Hill

This is the setting for the Cotswold 'Olympick Games', a version of which are still held in June each year. They no longer include such sporting delights as shin-kicking though! The hill provides the stadium. At the top is a viewpoint with topograph.

**Getting there:** North of Chipping Campden, off the B4035.

**Parking:** at the hill.

## Crickley Hill Country Park

58 hectares (144 acres) of beech woodland, grassland and park on the Cotswold escarpment. It is a site of archaeological interest and there is a visitor centre. Follow the waymarked trails for some grand views. Open daily, admission free.

**Getting there:** 4 miles south of Cheltenham on the B4070, near the junction with the A436.

**Parking:** in the park.

# *Bibliography*

*Walking in Haunted Gloucestershire* – Florence E. Jackson and Gordon Ottewell (Sigma Leisure)

*The Cotswolds* – Geoffrey N. Wright

*Gloucestershire Countryside* – Gordon Ottewell

*365 Days of Nature and Discovery* – Jane Reynolds

*Letts Pocket Guide to Butterflies* – Pamela Forey and Sue McCormick

*The Kingfisher Complete Guide to Wildlife of Britain and Europe* – ed. Michael Chinery

*Dorling Kindersley Children's Illustrated Encyclopaedia* – Dorling Kindersley.

*Wildlife Fact File; Cotswold Churches* – David Verey

*Minchinhampton and Avening* – A. T. Payne

*The Whittington Story* - Michael Whittington

# *Tourist Information Centres*

Cheltenham – Municipal Offices, The Promenade 01242 522878

Gloucester – St Michael's Tower, The Cross 01452 421188

Newent – The Library, High St. 01531 822145

Stow on the Wold – Hollis House, The Square 01451 831082

Tewkesbury – The Museum, Barton St. 01684 295027

Winchcombe – The Town Hall, High St. 01242 602925

# *Also of interest:*

## WALKING IN HAUNTED GLOUCESTERSHIRE

*Florence Jackson & Gordon Ottewell*

Gloucestershire is steeped in ghosts and famous hauntings. This is the perfect companion for those who dare to explore the supernatural side of this super county. Don't go on these walks alone!

*£6.95*

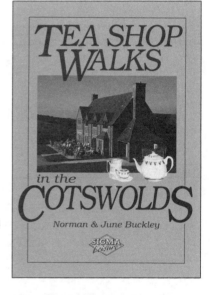

## TEA SHOP WALKS IN THE COTSWOLDS

*Norman & June Buckley*

No other area in Britain has as many tea shops as the Cotswolds. Here are 26 walks that visit all the popular towns and villages, averaging 5-6 miles and perfect for families. Each walk features a tea shop that welcomes walkers.

*£6.95*

All of our books are available from your local bookshop. In case of difficulty, or to obtain our complete catalogue, please contact:

**Sigma Leisure, 1 South Oak Lane, Wilmslow, Cheshire SK9 6AR**
**Phone: 01625 – 531035     Fax: 01625 – 536800**
**E-mail: sigma.press@zetnet.co.uk**

ACCESS and VISA orders welcome. Please add £2 p&p to all orders.